THE 1990 GENERAL ELECTIONS IN HAITI

Foreword by Jimmy Carter

**COUNCIL OF
FREELY-ELECTED
HEADS OF GOVERNMENT**

**NATIONAL DEMOCRATIC
INSTITUTE FOR
INTERNATIONAL AFFAIRS**

INTERNATIONAL DELEGATION
TO THE HAITIAN GENERAL ELECTIONS

December 16, 1990

JIMMY CARTER
Delegation Leader
Former President of the United States
Chairman, Council of Freely-Elected Heads of Government
United States

GEORGE PRICE
Delegation Co-Leader
Prime Minister, Belize; Vice
Chairman of the Council of
Freely-Elected Heads of
Government
Belize

JOHN C. WHITEHEAD
Delegation Co-Leader
Former Deputy Secretary of
State
United States

SERGIO AGUAYO
President, Academy of Human
Rights
Mexico

ESTEBAN CABALLERO
Director, Center for Democratic
Studies
Paraguay

GREGORIO ATIENZA
Former Secretary General,
NAMFREL
Philippines

ROSALYNN CARTER
Former First Lady
United States

FREDERICK BARTON
Former State Democratic Chair,
Maine
United States

BEN CLARE
Minister of State (Representing
Prime Minister Michael
Manley, Council Member)
Jamaica

LOVIDA H. COLEMAN, Esq.
Dilworth, Paxson, Kalish and
Kauffman
United States

ALFRED CUMMING
Legislative Assistant, Office of
Sen. Bob Graham
United States

DENZIL DOUGLAS, MP
Labour Party Leader
St. Kitts-Nevis

LARRY GARBER
NDI Senior Consultant for
Election Processes
United States

STEPHEN HORBLITT
Former Legislative Director,
Office of Rep. Walter Fauntroy
United States

LESTER HYMAN, Esq.
Swidler & Berlin
United States

LIONEL C. JOHNSON
NDI Senior Program Officer;
Haiti Program Manager
United States

HENRY KIMELMAN
Former U.S. Ambassador to
Haiti
United States

MARC LALONDE
Former Finance Minister
(Representing Former Prime
Minister Pierre Trudeau,
Council Member)
Canada

JENNIE LINCOLN
Associate Director, Latin
American and Caribbean
Program, Carter Center of
Emory University
United States

FRANCINE MARSHALL
House Subcommittee on
Western Hemisphere Affairs
United States

CHRISTOPHER MATHABE
Working Group on International
Relations, African National
Congress
South Africa

JENNIFER MCCOY
Carter Center and Georgia State
University
United States

SHELDON MCDONALD
Ministry of Foreign Affairs
Jamaica

ROBERT MCNAMARA
Former President of the World
Bank
United States

THE NATIONAL DEMOCRATIC INSTITUTE FOR INTERNATIONAL AFFAIRS

The National Democratic Institute for International Affairs (NDI) was established in 1983. By working with political parties and other institutions, NDI seeks to promote, maintain, and strengthen democratic institutions in new and emerging democracies. The Institute is chaired by former Vice President Walter F. Mondale and is headquartered in Washington, D.C.

NDI has conducted democratic development programs in more than 35 countries. Programs focus on six major areas:

Political Party Training: NDI conducts multipartisan training seminars in political development with a broad spectrum of democratic parties. NDI draws expert trainers from around the world to forums where members of fledgling parties learn first-hand the techniques of organization, communication and constituent contact.

Election Processes: NDI provides technical assistance for political parties and nonpartisan associations to conduct voter and civic education campaigns, and to organize election monitoring programs. The Institute has also organized more than 20 international observer delegations.

Legislative Training: In Eastern Europe, Latin American and Africa, NDI has organized legislative seminars focusing on legislative procedures, staffing, research information, constituent services and committee structures.

Local Government: Technical assistance on models of city management has been provided to national legislatures and municipal governments in Central and Eastern Europe and the Soviet Union.

Civil Military Relations: NDI brings together military and political leaders to promote dialogue and establish mechanisms for improving civil-military relations.

Civic Education: NDI supports and advises nonpartisan groups and political parties engaged in civic and voter education programs.

THE COUNCIL OF FREELY-ELECTED
HEADS OF GOVERNMENT

The Council of Freely Elected Heads of Government is an informal group of 19 former and current heads of government from throughout the Western Hemisphere. Established in November of 1986 at a meeting chaired by former U.S. Presidents Carter and Ford on "Reinforcing Democracy in Americas" at the Carter Center of Emory University, the Council's goal is to reinforce democracy and promote the peaceful resolution of conflict.

Members of the Council co-chaired a subsequent Consultation on the Hemispheric Agenda at the Carter Center in March 1989 that brought together government and business leaders of Latin America with U.S. government officials, including Secretary of State James A. Baker. An Executive Committee of Jimmy Carter (Chairman), Prime Minister George Price of Belize (Vice-Chairman), former President of Venezuela Rafael Caldera, and former President of Costa Rica Daniel Oduber have coordinated the Council's activities.

The headquarters of the Council is at the Carter Center's Latin American and Caribbean Program. Since its founding, the Council has undertaken activities to support democratic activities in Haiti (1987), Argentina (1987), Chile (1988), Panama (1989, Nicaragua (1989-90), the Dominican Republic (1990), and again in Haiti (1990).

TEAM DEPLOYMENT

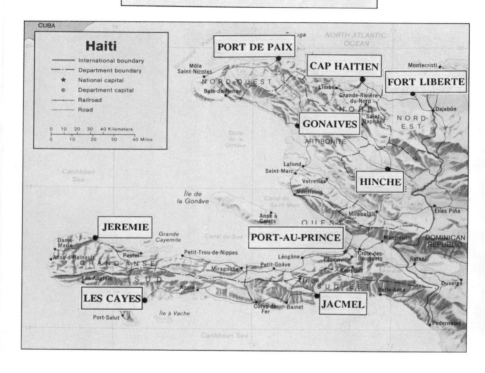

TABLE OF CONTENTS

ACKNOWLEDGEMENTS

This is the report of the international delegation that observed the December 16, 1990 general elections in Haiti. The report is based on information gathered by the delegation's sponsors - the Council of Freely-Elected Heads of Government, which is based at the Carter Center of Emory University, and the National Democratic Institute for International Affairs (NDI). The information used in preparing this report was collected before and after the elections, and by the delegation teams that visited the different cities and regions of Haiti on election day.

The report was prepared under the auspices of the two organizations, after consultations with members of the delegation. While these consultations indicate a consensus for the conclusions reached herein, the Council and NDI assume full responsibility for the accuracy of the report.

The report was drafted by NDI Senior Program Officer Lionel Johnson and edited by Dr. Robert Pastor, director of the Carter Center's Latin American and Caribbean Program, NDI President Brian Atwood, Executive Vice President Kenneth Wollack, Senior Consultant for Election Processes Larry Garber, and Public Information Director Sue Grabowski. Important contributions were made by NDI Program Specialist Gabe Hütter and NDI Advisor David Aasen.

The Council and NDI appreciate the assistance provided by the United States Agency for International Development that made the international observer delegation possible.

2

The international delegation extends warm appreciation to NDI Logistics Coordinator Leticia Martinez, Program Officers Donna Huffman and Sean Carroll, Program Assistants Gabe Hütter, Peter Silverman, Michael Ratner, and Amy Biehl, Executive Assistant Geraldine Thompson, and Intern Rodney Washington for their invaluable assistance in organizing the delegation and its activities. Special thanks for their support of the delegation are also extended to Carter Center staff members, including Jennie Lincoln, Associate Director of the Latin American and Caribbean Program; Dayle Powell Spencer, Director of the Conflict Resolution Program; and Karin Ryan, Acting Director of the Human Rights Program; and to Jennifer McCoy, Associate Professor at Georgia State University. Finally, the delegation also wishes to thank Carol Muldawer for her superb photography throughout the Council/NDI program.

May 1991

FOREWORD

The successful December 16, 1990 general elections in Haiti were not only an historic moment for that proud country, they were an opportunity for the entire hemisphere to celebrate. The journey of Haitians toward free and fair elections was long and arduous, and all citizens of an increasingly democratic hemisphere congratulate the Haitian people on this great achievement.

During most of Haiti's troubled history, a transition to democracy consistently eluded its people. As a country with almost no democratic traditions, the path toward elections in Haiti contained formidable obstacles and challenges. Although elections alone do not signal the arrival of democracy, in going to the polls on December 16 Haitians demonstrated to the world that they were prepared to take the critical first step toward economic and political development.

As Chairman of the Council of Freely-Elected Heads of Government, which is composed of 19 former and current hemispheric heads of government and is based at the Carter Center of Emory University, I was invited by Provisional President Ertha Pascal Trouillot, the Provisional Electoral Council and leaders of the major political parties to observe the December 1990 general elections. The National Democratic Institute for International Affairs (NDI) received similar invitations from Haiti's government and political leaders. NDI has extensive experience in monitoring and observing elections throughout the world, has conducted a comprehensive program of political development in Haiti since 1986, and observed the aborted November 1987 elections. The Council and NDI conducted an eight-month program in support of Haiti's election process, which included a series of monitoring missions focusing on security and other election issues. These efforts culminated in Council and NDI co-sponsorship of a 33-member international and bi-partisan delegation to observe the December elections and my own return for the inauguration of the new president in February.

Our December observer mission was fortunate to have as one of its co-leaders Prime Minister George Price of Belize, who is vice chairman of the Council. We have worked together in observing previous elections in Panama, Nicaragua and Haiti. We were honored to have John C. Whitehead, who was deputy secretary of state during the Reagan Administration, serve as our other co-leader. He made an invaluable contribution to our mission. I also had the pleasure of working with Mr. Whitehead in observing the historic elections in Nicaragua. I am extremely grateful to the other distinguished members of our delegation, who travelled from 12 nations to observe this truly momentous election process.

I owe special thanks to Lionel Johnson, NDI senior program officer, and Dr. Robert Pastor, director of the Carter Center's Latin American and Caribbean Program, for organizing the delegation. We also express appreciation to the Agency for International Development (AID) for a grant that made this mission possible.

The election report was drafted by Lionel Johnson and edited by Dr. Robert Pastor, with assistance from NDI President Brian Atwood, NDI Executive Vice President Kenneth Wollack, and others.

The December 1990 elections, while indeed an historic moment for Haiti, was only the first step toward a full democratic transition. Together with my wife Rosalynn and Dr. Robert Pastor, I returned to Haiti at the invitation of President-elect Jean-Bertrand Aristide to witness his inauguration on February 7, 1991. I was greatly impressed by the outpouring of support for the new president and his genuine interest in leading his people toward democracy and social justice. The support he has received from General Herard Abraham and the army is also encouraging.

The new government and the popular forces that support it have a unique opportunity and responsibility to establish the country's democratic institutions and work toward solving the economic, social and political problems of all Haitians within a constitutional framework. These improvements will not come about immediately and will require a truly national commitment, sacrifice and unity of purpose. We remain committed in our desire to help.

Jimmy Carter
May 1991

EXECUTIVE SUMMARY

A 33-member international and bipartisan delegation, organized by the Council of Freely-Elected Heads of Government and the National Democratic Institute for International Affairs (NDI), observed the general elections in the Republic of Haiti on December 16, 1990. An NDI team also returned to Haiti to observe the run-off elections on January 20, 1991, and President Carter led a small group to attend the inauguration of the new president on February 7, 1991. As set forth in the delegation's terms of reference, the elections were evaluated in three phases: the pre-election preparations and campaign environment; the balloting and counting processes; and the post-election formation of a new government. To realize this evaluation, the delegation relied upon the findings of pre-election survey and monitoring missions to Haiti in May, July, September, October and November 1990, as well as the observations of the delegation members during the period of the December elections and the January 1991 run-off.

On the day of Jean-Bertrand Aristide's inauguration as president, exactly five years had passed since the departure from Haiti of Jean-Claude Duvalier. During that interim period, a democratic transition had consistently eluded the people of Haiti. Seeking a way out of their country's political and economic impasse, Haitians went to the polls on December 16 to elect a new national government and local officials. As the Western Hemisphere's poorest nation and a country with few democratic traditions, Haiti experienced an election process plagued by obstacles and challenges. Haiti's last attempt at democratic elections on November 29, 1987 was aborted following a massacre of 34 innocent civilians, in which the military government was apparently complicit. The January 1988 elections, which resulted in Leslie Manigat's brief tenure as president, were widely believed to have been rigged by the military government. The military *juntas* that succeeded Manigat's government often pledged to hold elections, but never delivered on those promises.

Supreme Court Justice Ertha Pascal Trouillot assumed the presidency in March 1990 with a mandate to lead the country to free elections. In July, General Herard Abraham, the commander in chief of the armed forces, appointed a Security Coordinating Committee composed of colonels to coordinate security arrangements. The committee worked closely with the Provisional Electoral Council (CEP) and consulted with United Nations advisors in formulating a comprehensive security plan. Nonetheless, despite this plan and repeated assurances, on the eve of the elections, many Haitians remained wary of the armed forces' commitment to providing a secure election environment. With the memories of 1987 fresh in their minds, many Haitians feared that elements of the Duvalier regime might again disrupt the election process. A sharp increase in the number of violent incidents in mid-1990, including an armed attack on a meeting of the Council of State and a terrorist bombing at a campaign rally a week before the elections, contributed to doubts about the prospects for secure elections. The elections, however, proceeded without incident.

With some exceptions, the international community responded slowly to the Government of Haiti's request for election assistance, but by the time of the elections, hundreds of international observers, especially United Nations security and civilian personnel and Organization of American States (OAS) observers had arrived, giving Haitians added confidence to vote. At the invitation of the Haitian government, the Council of Freely-Elected Heads of Government and NDI jointly sponsored a series of pre-election monitoring missions focusing on security issues and the administrative preparations for the polls, as well as the December observer delegation. (See Appendix I.)

By participating in these elections, Haitians demonstrated their commitment to setting their nation on a course toward democratic development and prosperity. The following are the delegation's summary conclusions regarding the election process:

1) The people of Haiti voted in record numbers to express their desire for democratic change. While administratively problematic, the elections were the nation's freest and represent a milestone in Haiti's history. The overwhelming popular mandate given to Jean-Bertrand Aristide expressed the people's desire to break with Haiti's history of authoritarian rule and economic stagnation.

2) In contrast to the aborted November 1987 elections, the government of Haiti supported the election process. Provisional President Ertha Pascal Trouillot, operating under extremely difficult circumstances, maintained a commitment to the election process and ensured that the government remained neutral regarding the process. President Trouillot invited the UN, the OAS and other international organizations to observe the elections. This international presence contributed greatly in providing confidence to the electorate.

Led by Chief of Staff General Herard Abraham, the armed forces played a pivotal role in the process by ensuring a secure election environment. There is cause for hope that the armed forces will continue this constructive and constitutional role.

Finally, the Provisional Electoral Council (CEP) labored against tremendous odds to ensure the people of Haiti an opportunity to participate in a meaningful and credible election process. The CEP set a very positive precedent for the role that a permanent election commission should play under Haiti's 1987 Constitution in administering future elections.

3) The election environment was far from perfect. Several incidents of violence occurred during the pre-election period, which resulted in numerous fatalities and injuries. There were genuine concerns on the part of the electorate as to whether the armed forces would support the election process and whether voters would have enough confidence to participate. To counter the skepticism throughout the pre-election period, the Council and NDI stressed a basic, but essential, theme — that the election process must go forward.

Despite the aforementioned security problems, most candidates and parties reported no serious complaints of bias directed against them during the campaign period, and believed they were afforded an ample opportunity to communicate their respective messages to the public through rallies, the media, posters and other activities. On balance, the campaign was conducted in a remarkably peaceful manner.

4) The elections posed tremendous administrative challenges. Within a relatively short time frame, the Election Council had to register voters, prepare and distribute ballots and other paraphernalia for five elections, designate and train polling officials responsible for administering more than 14,000 polling sites, and make several critical political decisions as mandated by the constitution. Despite the problems that emerged, including potentially explosive ones related to the delay in distributing ballots on election day, the CEP and all election officials are to be complimented for their successful and courageous efforts in the conduct of the election process.

5) While there were delays in the transmission and tabulation of official results, the parallel vote tabulation conducted jointly by the UN and the OAS provided timely information to the CEP, the government, the political parties and ultimately the public regarding the outcome. This alleviated some of the tension that may have emerged as a consequence of the delays in announcing the official results.

6) The delegation wishes to congratulate the people of Haiti, who have waited so long to participate in a meaningful election. The Haitian people overcame what for many were quite real fears of violence and intimidation to cast their ballots. The elections, which marked an historic moment for Haiti, are merely the beginning of the long and arduous process of building a truly democratic system.

The forces of democratic change now have a tremendous opportunity and responsibility to improve the lives of the people of Haiti. They deserve the respect, admiration and support of the community of nations. In responding to the challenges facing a poor country with limited democratic traditions, the new president and his administration will require the assistance and support of many people within and outside Haiti.

INTRODUCTION

This report assesses the 1990 general elections in Haiti from the vantage point of the 33-member international observer delegation co-sponsored by the Council of Freely-Elected Heads of Government and the National Democratic Institute for International Affairs (NDI). Prior to the December observer mission, the Council and NDI co-sponsored a series of monitoring missions that focused on the Haitian government's preparations for the elections and on the issue of security.

By demonstrating international support for democracy in Haiti, the international delegation sought, by its presence, to contribute to a peaceful election environment and to encourage a high voter turnout. Despite some initial and understandable skepticism, most Haitians came to realize that the December 16 elections could signal the beginning of their country's future development. Moreover, they understood that the international community would have to view the elections as a truly democratic exercise in order for desperately needed economic development assistance to resume.

The Council/NDI monitoring effort was part of a larger role played by the international community in supporting Haiti's quest for democracy. The strong commitment of the UN, the OAS, the Organization of Eastern Caribbean States (CARICOM), the United States, Canada, Venezuela and other nations helped to ensure that this chance for democracy was Haiti's best.

In the final analysis however, the people of Haiti, through their courage and determination, ensured the success of the December 16 elections. It was clear that, in the face of adversity, Haitians wanted to move their nation forward. The 1990 elections were Haiti's freest and provide President Jean-Bertrand Aristide a broad popular mandate for democratic change.

The first chapter of this report describes Council and NDI activities in support of Haiti's election process. Chapters two and three present a brief historical and constitutional overview. Chapter four discusses the electoral environment. The fifth chapter provides the delegation's election-day observations, while the sixth chapter describes the counting process, the January 20, 1991 run-off elections and the inauguration. The seventh chapter offers some reflections on Haiti's election process.

Chapter 1

COUNCIL AND NDI ELECTION ACTIVITIES IN HAITI

The Council of Freely-Elected Heads of Government and the National Democratic Institute for International Affairs recognize that the promotion of free and fair elections requires more than merely dispatching an observer delegation to a country on election day. Given Haiti's previously tenuous democratic traditions, it was evident from the outset that a much more extensive commitment in support of Haitian democracy was necessary to help ensure the success of the December elections.

In committing to support the 1990 Haitian elections, neither the Council nor NDI had any illusions regarding the formidable challenges facing the Haitian government and its people in realizing these elections. Plans for meeting the challenges included: 1) establishing voter confidence in the government's commitment to free and fair elections; 2) encouraging participation in the process by conveying the message that the elections would be a critical first step on the road toward Haiti's political maturation; 3) guaranteeing security throughout the country during the entire election process, thereby permitting unhampered voter participation in each of its phases; and 4) providing adequate financial and logistical support for the overall election process. In overcoming these obstacles, the Haitian government would rely heavily on assistance from external sources.

A. Pre-1990 Council/NDI Activities

The Council and NDI have supported Haiti's democratic development since the immediate post-Duvalier period. In August 1986, NDI sponsored a seminar on "The Role of Political Parties in the Transitional State," in San Juan, Puerto Rico. Prompted by this program, Haitian political leaders called for the creation of an independent electoral commission. This proposal was the precursor of the Provisional Electoral Council (CEP) established by Haiti's 1987 Constitution. In March 1987, an NDI team observed the successful constitutional referendum and, in June of that year, conducted a political party-building seminar in Port-au-Prince.

In October 1987, President Jimmy Carter and Prime Minister George Price of Belize led a Council/NDI mission intended to help put Haiti's election process back on track following the assassination of presidential candidate Yves Volel. In November 1987, Prime Minister Price and NDI President Brian Atwood led an international observer delegation to the general elections, which were subsequently aborted due to violence. The delegation's report on the election process, which condemned the failure of the interim government to provide security on election day, was published subsequently by NDI.

B. 1990 Pre-Election Missions

1. May 1990 survey mission

The Council/NDI program in support of the 1990 elections in Haiti resulted from the recommendations of an NDI survey team, led by Senior Program Officer Lionel Johnson, that visited Port-au-Prince from May 20-24, and subsequently by an invitation from Provisional President Ertha Pascal Trouillot to President Carter and NDI. During the May survey visit, the team met with President Trouillot, Armed Forces Chief of Staff Herard Abraham, members of the CEP, Interior Minister Joseph Maxi, and a broad range of political and civic leaders.

At the time, President Trouillot said her sole political mandate was to lead Haiti to free elections. Trouillot harbored no presidential ambitions, and was committed to leaving the presidency as soon as feasible. Trouillot repeatedly expressed confidence in General Abraham and the armed forces' ability to provide a secure environment in which to conduct national elections. During the NDI team's visit however, it became unmistakably clear that this confidence was not shared by most of President Trouillot's fellow citizens; the memory of the aborted 1987 elections was still vivid in the minds of most Haitians.

The nine-member CEP was, at the time, reviewing the election law and establishing the electoral calendar. A decision had been made to reregister the entire electorate, and the CEP was also grappling with the issue of what form the election ballots would take. There was great concern that the large number of presidential and legislative candidates might make a unitary ballot confusing to the largely illiterate Haitian electorate. Many believed that it would be preferable to utilize, as had been done in 1987, color-coded party-specific ballots, which would bear numeric or party symbols easily identified by voters. International donors had agreed to provide the technical assistance necessary to support the voter registration effort.

The CEP was also revisiting the issue of participation by Duvalierists in the elections; Article 291 of the constitution prohibited the candidacy of any person who had been an "architect" of the Duvalier dictatorship, had practiced torture, or had extorted public funds. This did not necessarily preclude a candidacy by someone who had served in the Duvalier government. Some political leaders preferred to permit one or two such candidates to compete in the elections, believing that their defeat (in free and fair elections) would be assured. The CEP's deliberations on this issue were expected to have a direct impact on the electoral behavior of Duvalierists and other right-wing elements.

The CEP was acutely aware of the public's deep concern over the issue of election security. In response to these concerns, the CEP was considering the establishment of an "electoral police" force, which might be trained by the UN, OAS, CARICOM, or others. These unarmed volunteers would augment the presence of the armed forces at polling sites across the country. In addition, the CEP believed that the presence of numerous international observers would help guarantee secure and credible elections.

Beyond the task of crafting the election mechanism, the government faced the task of restoring voter confidence in its ability to provide a peaceful election environment. The NDI team was told by many Haitians that they had no intention of participating in the election process, regardless of the presence of troops and observers. During its meeting with General Abraham, the NDI team received assurances that the armed forces would respect the constitution, fully support the election process and provide necessary security measures. Abraham pointed to significant changes since the 1987 elections. For the first time since the departure of Jean-Claude Duvalier, the armed forces were truly subordinate to the civilian government, and approximately 1,000 pro-Duvalier and other right-wing elements of the armed forces had been removed in recent months.

Despite these assurances, there remained the widespread perception that the army could not be trusted, and that its commander in chief could not control his forces. The NDI team reported to General Abraham that the Haitian people appeared to be looking for gestures from the military to demonstrate its commitment to the restoration of democracy. These included the arrests and trials of those military officials believed to have been involved in the tragic events of November 29, 1987, and subsequent acts of wanton violence. Only through tangible deeds could the armed forces under General Abraham's command redeem themselves in the eyes of the public.

The NDI team found the political parties prepared to field candidates at the presidential, legislative and local levels. A common theme expressed by each leader was the need to restore voter confidence in a secure election process. Several of the potential presidential candidates, through media interviews, were encouraging Haitian voters to give democracy "one last chance."

The NDI team concluded that while the challenges to establishing democracy in Haiti were numerous, there was unquestionably a glimmer of hope that free and fair elections could be conducted. For the first time since Duvalier's exile, a civilian president committed to holding peaceful elections was in the presidential palace. Although criticized by some for timidity, President Trouillot had begun to respond to the challenge. Haitians appeared to want elections and hoped for economic development that could occur only after political stability was restored.

Based on the above findings, the NDI team recommended that the Council of Freely-Elected Heads of Government and the National Democratic Institute co-sponsor a series of pre-election monitoring missions to focus on preparations for the elections, including election security, and explore the feasibility of sending an observer delegation at the time of the elections. The team also recommended that NDI develop a comprehensive program to support the development of Haiti's political parties. Former President Carter had already been contacted by numerous Haitian leaders, including President Trouillot, and after consulting with other members of the Council, he agreed to lead an exploratory mission.

2. *July 1990 monitoring mission*

On July 25-26, President Carter, leading a Council/NDI delegation, visited Haiti to demonstrate the international community's support for Haiti's election process. The delegation included: former Canadian Finance Minister Marc Lalonde, representing Council member Pierre Trudeau; Barbados' Chief Electoral Officer Dennis Smith, representing Council member Erskine Sandiford; the Director of the Carter Center's Latin America and Caribbean Program Robert Pastor; and NDI Senior Program Officer Lionel Johnson. The delegation met with Haitian government and civic leaders and evaluated the prospects for a secure election environment during the general elections, which at the time, were scheduled for November 4, 1990. (See Appendix II.)

The delegation's visit came at a critical juncture, as issues relating to election security remained of prime concern. These issues were complicated by the return to Haiti a few weeks earlier of Roger Lafontant, the former interior minister and leader of the notorious *tontons macoutes*, and Williams Régala, a senior army officer and member of the army *junta* in place at the time of the violence against voters during the November 1987 elections. During its visit, the delegation explained that the international community would have to view the elections as a truly democratic exercise in order for economic development assistance to resume.

At the delegation's meeting with President Trouillot, she expressed again her firm commitment to the election process. She acknowledged, however, that the presence of Lafontant and Régala hampered her government's ability to allay fears that it would be unable to provide adequate security, and that a repeat of the November 1987 tragedy was possible. Trouillot reaffirmed her confidence in General Abraham and his commitment to executing the arrest warrant that had been issued for Lafontant. President Trouillot also was engaged in a political struggle with the Council of State (with which she shared executive power), contributing to the perception of passivity that had plagued her government from the outset.

President Carter told Trouillot that he thought the international community would respond favorably to Haiti's request for election assistance, despite some confusion regarding the request to the United Nations Security Council. Haiti sought a small number of security "advisors" who would work directly with Haiti's Armed Forces Security Coordinating Committee (SCC), and a team of UN election observers. (See Appendix III.) President Carter said he would personally urge UN Secretary General Javier Perez de Cuellar to secure UN approval of Haiti's request. Carter also said he would encourage the OAS and CARICOM to provide election assistance as soon as possible.

The delegation's meeting with General Abraham focused on election security and the army's efforts to apprehend Lafontant and Régala. Abraham said he was concerned that the presence of these two men might divert public attention from the important task of conducting the elections. In response to instructions from President Trouillot after her telephone conversation with President Carter, General Abraham offered a military helicopter to deliver a message from Carter to Lafontant encouraging him to leave Haiti. The mission was aborted, however, when Lafontant's associates refused to identify his location. The delegation also met with the SCC, which had been recently appointed by Abraham to oversee election security matters. President Carter and the delegation urged the SCC members, who were colonels close to General Abraham, to establish a budget and work plan, and begin its liaison activities with the CEP as soon as possible.

CEP President Jean Robert Sabalat outlined the CEP's plan for administering the elections, including the task of reregistering the electorate. Sabalat repeated the now familiar concerns regarding election security and said he looked forward to developing a sound working relationship with the SCC.

In the meeting with the delegation, members of the Council of State were extremely critical of Trouillot and her government. The Council had called on Trouillot to arrest Lafontant and Régala and bring to justice those responsible for the June 21 armed attack on the Council of State's meeting at the Hotel Santos, which resulted in the death of one of the Council's members. Council President Louis Roy, a noted human rights advocate, decried the fact that the nation appeared to be moving toward "elections at any cost," and some Council members categorically declared their intention to boycott the elections.

Most of Haiti's political leaders remained committed to participating in the election process, although a few declared that they could not do so "under present circumstances." The delegation strongly urged the political leaders to move forward with the elections and to condemn the use of violence during the process.

At the delegation's departure press conference, Carter said that free elections in Haiti would not be possible "unless clear and concrete measures were adopted to assure the complete security of all voters." The onus, therefore, was on Trouillot and the armed forces to guarantee an election environment free of violence, fear and intimidation. There was recognition, however, that the government lacked the resources to accomplish this alone, and the delegation encouraged the international community to answer Haiti's urgent call for assistance. On his return, Carter wrote to the secretaries general of the UN and OAS, urging a positive response to the Haitian request for civilian and security election observers.

3. July 1990 NDI party-building seminar

NDI convened a two-day seminar on the "Role of Political Parties in an Electoral Process" July 27-29, immediately following the Council/NDI monitoring mission. The seminar brought together three mid-level members from each of seven prominent political parties in Haiti. They were joined by international experts who shared their experience and expertise on election monitoring: Genaro Arriagada, vice president of the Christian Democratic Party of Chile; Gregorio Atienza, former secretary general of the National Citizens Movement for Fair Elections (NAMFREL) of the Philippines; Grozdan Karadjov, organizing secretary of the Bulgarian Association for Free Elections; Esteban Caballero, director of the Center for Democratic Studies of Paraguay; Frederick Barton, former Democratic Party chairman of the state of Maine; and NDI political advisor Glenn Cowan. These experts shared their knowledge and experience of electoral processes with the party organizers. NDI Executive Vice President Kenneth Wollack and Senior Program Officer Lionel Johnson led the seminar proceedings. The program's workshops and one-on-one consultations dealt specifically with issues of voter participation, party pollwatching and independent vote counting.

A direct outcome of the seminar was the establishment of the Haitian Association for Free Elections (AHPEL). The participating parties agreed at the conclusion of the seminar to pool resources for a party-based association with the objectives of increasing voter participation and ensuring the free and fair conduct of the elections through voter education programs and party pollwatching activities. NDI continued working with AHPEL throughout the election process and sponsored training workshops for AHPEL activists in support of the association's objectives.

4. *September 1990 monitoring mission*

President Carter led a second Council/NDI mission to Haiti from September 20-22. The immediate goal was to move forward the country's election process, which had stalled. The delegation included Rosalynn Carter, Venezuela's Vice Minister of the Presidency Beatrice Rangel, Robert Pastor and Lionel Johnson. Prior to the visit, Carter consulted with Prime Minister Michael Manley in Jamaica and President Carlos Andres Perez in Venezuela. The two leaders agreed to use their influence to build international support for the elections. (See Appendix IV.)

Immediately prior to the delegation's visit, Haiti's political leadership had again become deeply divided over whether general elections could or should be held in the fall. There was a widespread perception that President Trouillot and General Abraham were slow in addressing the election security issues. Roger Lafontant and Williams Régala remained at large, and violence was on the rise throughout the country. Moreover, the stalemate continued between Trouillot and Council of State President Roy, and all official dialogue between the two executive branch partners had ceased.

Many Haitians had also begun to doubt the international community's willingness to support the election process. The U.S. Senate decision in August to deny non-lethal assistance to Haiti's military, coupled with the UN Security Council's failure to respond to Haiti's request for security assistance, contributed to this uncertainty. On September 14, President Trouillot sent a second request to the UN Secretary General for security support.

The Council/NDI delegation sought to encourage agreement by Haiti's leaders that the process of democratic transition would begin only through the conduct of free elections. It reiterated that further postponement of the process would exacerbate tensions in Haiti, and create concerns within the international community that the election process was no longer on track. Nevertheless, many in Haiti were more skeptical than ever that successful elections would take place.

President Carter and the delegation encouraged everyone with whom they spoke to recommit themselves to moving forward with the election process. Soon after the delegation's meeting with the CEP, a revised election calendar was published, providing for a registration program beginning October 5, with general elections planned for December 16. Although questions regarding election funding and other logistical concerns remained, the CEP launched the registration drive as scheduled. The CEP told the delegation that it was encouraged by the improved dialogue and cooperation with the armed forces SCC.

President Trouillot told the delegation she was deeply concerned about the country's grave fiscal crisis, and said that a democratic election was an essential precondition to reinvigorating the Haitian economy. Delegation member Beatrice Rangel replied that the Venezuelan government was prepared to grant Haiti favorable terms in the purchase of badly needed oil, and she returned to Caracas with a Haitian government delegation to conclude such an agreement.

It appeared that the impasse between Trouillot and the Council of State would not be broken in the near term. Council President Roy remained highly critical of Trouillot for allegedly violating the terms of their executive power-sharing arrangement, but also appeared to be seeking ways to ease the Council away from its anti-elections posture.

In sessions with labor leaders, human rights activists and political party leaders, the delegation stressed that the momentum in favor of the elections seemed to be increasing. The highlight of the delegation's visit was a trip to Gonaives, the economically distressed port city that has been a flash point in Haitian political struggles since independence. The delegation met with local military and civilian officials, as well as political, business, religious and human rights leaders. Support for the election process in the city appeared to be genuine. President Carter briefly addressed a crowd of approximately 2,000 Gonaives residents and encouraged them to register to vote during the coming weeks. Mr. Carter's remarks were greeted with overwhelming enthusiasm.

Following his visit to Haiti, President Carter consulted with numerous international political leaders to garner support in the United Nations for Haiti's request for security and civilian observers and to gain economic aid for the elections. Venezuelan President Perez won the support of the other Andean countries, and Jamaican Prime Minister Manley helped mobilize CARICOM. President Carter also wrote an op-ed article on the Haitian elections for the *New York Times*, urging the United Nations and other nations to support the elections. (See Appendix V.) On October 5, the United Nations General Assembly passed a resolution requesting the Secretary General to provide support to Haiti for the elections. (See Appendix VI.)

5. *October 1990 monitoring missions*

Midway through the voter registration process, President Carter, Rosalynn Carter, Jamaica's Minister of State Ben Clare and Robert Pastor briefly visited Haiti on October 12 to encourage Haitians to register to vote. From October 16-19, another Council/NDI delegation, led by Prime Minister George Price, also travelled to Haiti to support the registration process. The delegation included: Andrew Young, former Mayor of Atlanta and U.S. Ambassador to the United Nations; Beatrice Rangel; Denzil Douglas, Labour Party Leader of St. Kitts/Nevis; Esteban Caballero; and Lionel Johnson. The delegation met with government, political and civic leaders in Port-au-Prince, and journeyed to the northern coast city of Cap Haitien to observe the registration process there. (See Appendix VII for arrival statement.)

It became clear that despite some logistical problems, Haitians were registering to vote in record numbers, indicating increased confidence in the election process. To accommodate a last-minute surge in registration, the CEP agreed to extend the registration period by a few days.

6. *November 1990 pre-election survey mission*

Lionel Johnson and NDI advisor Glenn Cowan visited Haiti in late November to assess final preparations for the December 16 elections. During meetings with CEP officials, Johnson and Cowan learned of the formidable task of training CEP pollwatchers and conducting voter education programs. It was clear that the voting and counting processes on election day would severely tax the CEP's limited resources. It would be extremely difficult just to deliver the ballots to all of Haiti's 12,000-15,000 polling sites, or electoral bureaus (BIVs), by election day, as some areas could be reached only on horseback. Despite these problems, officials of the CEP exhibited resolve during the final phase of the pre-election period to see through this enormously important task to a successful conclusion.

C. December 13-17 Election Observation Mission

The Council/NDI international observer delegation assembled in Port-au-Prince on December 14. (See Appendices VIIIa and VIIIb.) The delegation received briefings on election procedures from representatives of the CEP, the armed forces, and the UN and OAS observer teams. The armed forces report was especially encouraging, as it indicated full cooperation by the army and police with election officials. There was, nonetheless, some degree of concern within the delegation that the enormous logistical problems and security threats from Duvalierist elements would not permit orderly elections.

On the morning of December 15, most of the delegation teams left Port-au-Prince to be deployed in Haiti's eight other political subdivisions or departments. (See Appendix IX.) The delegation members who remained in the capital called on President Trouillot and General Abraham. They also met with several of the presidential candidates, none of whom had any serious complaints about the electoral process. The candidates especially complimented the army and the police for their cooperation and for providing security during the campaign.

On election day, the observer teams were at polling sites by 6 a.m. Few sites were ready for voters at that time, but most opened within an hour or two. A few sites in Port-au-Prince, notably in Cité Soleil (an area where Jean-Bertrand Aristide was very popular), did not receive ballots or election materials in the morning. By early afternoon, the assembled crowds were becoming quite hostile. After consulting with the OAS and UN observer missions and receiving reports from other areas outside of the capital, the Council/NDI team in Port-au-Prince judged that the problem in Cité Soleil was an isolated one, and that most BIVs were functioning normally.

The Port-au-Prince observer group then divided into four teams. One led by President Carter went to the CEP headquarters to report on the problems and to try to expedite the delivery of election materials. Another group, which included Prime Minister George Price, Andrew Young, Jim Wright, Robert McNamara, John Whitehead and Robert Pastor, visited Aristide to report that the problem in Cité Soleil was serious but appeared to be unusual, and that President Carter was meeting with the CEP to try to facilitate the delivery of election materials. The group encouraged Aristide to calm his supporters so that violence could not be used as a pretext by groups opposed to free elections to abort them. The group promised Aristide that together with the OAS and the UN, the Council/NDI delegation members would be in a position to judge whether the elections were free or rigged, and if they were free, the delegation would offer strong support to the victor. If the elections were rigged, the observers would denounce them.

One of the delegation members asked Father Aristide if he would respect the results of free elections if he were not the winner. He insisted that he would win and, if he didn't, it followed that the elections were rigged. Aristide asked the group why he was being asked such a question. The group responded that it had asked the same question of all the candidates, but that Aristide was the only one who did not unequivocally agree to accept the results of elections deemed fair by the international observers. The delegation members all tried to reassure Aristide that the delegation would support the results of a free and fair process, and urge international assistance for the Haitian economy.

Aristide's reports of election day developments differed from those of the delegation. He said the situation at Cité Soleil was typical of a larger effort to deny the people of Haiti free elections. The group said that if Aristide's reports were accurate, the

Council/NDI delegation would definitely condemn the elections, but insisted that it was too soon to draw conclusions about the process.

At CEP headquarters, President Carter encouraged the CEP to use the media to assure voters that everyone would be given the opportunity to vote no matter how long it might take. By late afternoon, the ballots had arrived at all polling sites, and some voters from Cité Soleil had been permitted to vote at alternative sites.

In the evening, the delegation teams observed the orderly conclusion of voting and the counting of ballots. By about midnight, the OAS and UN "quick count" confirmed the impressions and the informal survey of the delegation: Aristide had won the election by a landslide — a *lavelas* — with about two-thirds of the vote.

The next morning, the delegation teams reassembled in the capital for a debriefing session. The delegation teams reported that the election results appeared to be uniform nationwide, and that the process was generally orderly throughout the country. For example, the team that observed the voting in the southern city of Les Cayes reported that "in terms of the spirit and intent of the guidelines, the process was largely faultless." Many of the delegation teams reported a variety of minor election law violations: lack of voter secrecy; campaigning near some polling sites; and failure to use indelible ink in some instances.

President and Mrs. Carter visited Trouillot and Abraham to congratulate them on their success in ensuring a peaceful election. At a mid-day news conference, the delegation issued a statement congratulating Trouillot, the armed forces, the CEP and the people of Haiti. (See Appendices Xa and Xb.)

President and Mrs. Carter, Prime Minister Price, John Whitehead, Robert Pastor and Lionel Johnson then visited Aristide and congratulated him on his victory. Aristide thanked President Carter for all that he and the delegation had done to ensure free elections. He acknowledged that the reports he had received the day before had been inaccurate. Pastor said that Aristide had been correct about the outcome of the elections, and that the Council/NDI delegation had been accurate about the process. President Carter pledged his full support for the new government and said that all of the members of the delegation promised to help as well. Father Aristide expressed his gratitude for their support and eagerness to continue working closely with them. He then invited President Carter to return for the inauguration.

The group visited the runner-up in the presidential election, Marc Bazin, commended him on running a good campaign, and encouraged him to continue playing a constructive role in the future. Bazin accepted his defeat gracefully and said that he would make a statement at the appropriate time after the official election results were announced by the CEP. He also expressed willingness to work with the new government should they invite him to join.

D. January 20, 1991 Run-off

An NDI team travelled to Haiti January 17-21 to observe the run-off elections and to demonstrate the Council and NDI's continued commitment to Haitian democracy. The team included: Lionel Johnson; Stephen Horblitt, former legislative director to U. S. Representative Walter Fauntroy; and NDI Program Assistants Gabe Hütter and Michael Ratner. During the visit, the team met with officials of the CEP and the OAS, as well as political and civic leaders, and observed the polling in Port-au-Prince, its outlying areas, the southern port city of Jacmel, and many polling stations in between.

E. The Inauguration of February 7, 1991

President and Mrs. Carter and Robert Pastor returned to Haiti for the inauguration of President Aristide on February 7, 1991, five years after the departure of Jean-Claude Duvalier. On the evening before, they met with Venezuelan President Perez, Prime Minister Manley and Prime Minister Price.

The president was sworn in at the Parliament. The new leaders of the Senate and the Chamber of Deputies indicated their interest in establishing the independence of their institutions while at the same time working closely with the new president to improve the lives of the Haitian people. President Aristide delivered his inaugural address in front of the National Palace, during which he underscored his desire to work closely with the army to protect the people and to seek the help and cooperation of all nations. (See Appendix XI.)

Chapter 2

HISTORICAL BACKGROUND

A. From Discovery to U.S. Occupation*

The tragic pattern of Haiti's history can be traced back to the nation's origins. Discovered by Christopher Columbus for Spain in 1492, Haiti, which forms the western third of the island of Hispaniola, was ceded to France in 1697 as part of the Treaty of Ryswick. The French established sugar and coffee plantations, and by the 1770s Haiti had become the wealthiest of France's colonies in the Caribbean. A small minority of whites, as well as free mulattos and blacks, profited from the labor of the 500,000 slaves who worked on the plantations.

In 1791, the slaves revolted, thus launching a long struggle with France. In 1804, Haiti emerged as the hemisphere's second independent republic and the world's first independent black nation. The cost of the revolution was devastating. About one-third of the former slave population died during the course of the fighting, and the country's profitable agricultural base was destroyed. Throughout the 19th century, civil wars and a succession of dictators who plundered Haiti's diminishing wealth ensured the stagnation of the country's economy. Haiti became a land of largely illiterate, black, Creole-speaking smallholders who lived in isolation from the mulatto-dominated towns. Effective government was nonexistent, and Haiti's

---

* The material in this section is largely drawn from Robert I. Rotberg, *Haiti: The Politics of Squalor*, Boston: Houghton Mifflin, 1971.

regimes became increasingly unstable and short-lived. Of the 22 Haitian presidents who held office between 1843 and 1915, 14 were overthrown, one resigned, three were murdered, three died of natural causes in office, and only one finished his term.

By the beginning of the 20th century, Haiti was deeply in debt to French, German, and U.S. financial interests. In July 1915, the U.S. government, concerned about civil unrest in Haiti, sent the Marine Corps to occupy the country. The Marines maintained law and order, but no real attempt was made to prepare Haiti for democratic government. In 1934, soon after the Americans left, Haiti reverted to a dictatorship. In the years following the occupation, the army emerged as the kingmaker in Haitian politics, eventually installing one of its own, General Paul Magloire, as president in 1950.

B. The Duvalier Era: 1957-1986

Magloire's fall in December 1956 was followed by five military dictatorships in 10 months and, finally, national elections. Thirteen candidates entered the presidential race at the beginning of a volatile, nine-month campaign. In the end, the contest was between Louis Déjoie, a wealthy mulatto senator, and the last remaining black candidate, François "Papa Doc" Duvalier, a former minister for public health who had the backing of the army. Notwithstanding allegations of voter intimidation and fraud in the countryside, Duvalier and his party won a massive victory. Official results gave Duvalier 679,884 votes to Déjoie's 266,993. In addition, Duvalierists swept the Senate, and Déjoie's party won only one seat in the House.

François Duvalier became president on October 22, 1957. The humble image of a modest country doctor, which Duvalier had fostered during the election campaign, soon proved deceptive. Within a year, he began ruling by decree, while his private militia, the *tontons macoutes*, extorted money from all sectors of the population, suppressed opposition voices, and generally spread terror throughout the country. In 1964, Duvalier declared himself president-for-life. During the ensuing five years, at least a half-million Haitians, among them the majority of Haiti's professionals, left their country for the Dominican Republic, the United States and Canada.

Upon François Duvalier's death in 1971, his 19-year-old son, Jean-Claude "Baby Doc", assumed the presidency. The younger Duvalier lacked his father's excessive temper and at times seemed willing to accept the idea of limited political reform. International financial assistance, especially from the United States, was modest during the 1970s, and efforts made by the United States government to compel Duvalier to enact meaningful reforms were unsuccessful. In late November 1980, following a crackdown on the opposition and massive arrests, a new wave of refugees fled the country, many arriving in boats on the shores of Florida and the Bahamas.

In the early 1980s, Jean-Claude Duvalier's political and economic strategy followed a singular pattern. Promises of political reform and bogus democratic displays designed to appease foreign (primarily U.S.) donors alternated with acts of political repression. During national elections held in February 1984, Duvalier's candidates, running unopposed, swept both houses of the legislature.

In November 1985, the Haitian army killed several protesters at an anti-government demonstration in Gonaives. Protests spread to the rest of the country and continued through January 1986. Finally, on February 7, Duvalier and his family, responding to entreaties from the United States, Jamaica and other countries, left Haiti for France on board a U.S. military aircraft.

C. The First Year After Duvalier

Before leaving Haiti, Jean-Claude Duvalier transferred all powers of government to a six-member Council of National Government (CNG). The CNG was headed by General Henri Namphy and included Colonels Williams Régala and Prosper Avril; all three had served under the Duvaliers. With this arrangement, the army regained some of the prominence it had lost during the Duvalier era. In March 1986, following renewed protests and the resignation of Gerard Gourge, a prominent human rights advocate and one of the

CNG's civilian members, Namphy announced a new version of the Council, consisting of Namphy, Régala and civilian Jacques François.

In June 1986, Namphy announced a timetable for local and national elections. In October, with most prominent democrats remaining on the sidelines in protest of what they perceived to be bogus elections, a Constituent Assembly was elected to draft a new constitution. Rejecting preliminary draft proposals by the CNG and the ministry of the interior, the Assembly prepared an entirely new constitution, which was overwhelmingly ratified in a referendum held in March 1987. It called for: 1) the establishment of an impartial, nonmilitary Provisional Electoral Council (CEP) to supervise the upcoming elections; 2) a reduction of the executive's powers and the simultaneous restoration and expansion of the powers of the legislature and the judiciary; and 3) the exclusion of individuals associated with the Duvalier regime from public office for 10 years (Article 291).

D. The Aborted 1987 Elections

The CEP was established in May 1987. In accordance with the new constitution, the CEP's nine members were drawn from different sectors of Haitian society. Tension between the CNG and the CEP erupted in June, when the CNG refused to promulgate the election law drafted by the CEP and instead published an election law that provided the CEP with only limited authority. Bowing to public outcry, the CNG revoked its election law in August and promulgated the CEP's law with a few insignificant changes.

Meanwhile, incidents of violence in connection with the scheduled November elections increased. These included the assassinations of presidential candidates Louis Eugène Athis and Yves Volel. In all, more than 100 Haitians were killed during the months prior to the elections. The CNG was widely accused of condoning the violence, which was generally presumed to be the work of Duvalierists. On November 3 pursuant to Article 291 of the constitution, following the CEP's rejection of the candidacies of several individuals involved with the Duvalier regime, the CEP's offices were burned down. Despite the fire and threats, the CEP continued with its preparations for the presidential and legislative elections, although few expected the elections to be administered without significant problems.

On the morning of election day, November 29, shootings took place at a number of polling stations in Port-au-Prince and around the country. Thirty-four people were killed. Three hours after the opening of the polls, in an attempt to avert further violence, the CEP canceled the elections. General Namphy, appearing on television that night, blamed the CEP for the failure of the elections and criticized foreign observers for interfering with the electoral process. Most observers, including an international delegation sponsored by NDI, later reported that the armed forces and the police, who were responsible for the security of the elections, had tolerated and in some cases even participated in the violence. The NDI delegation encouraged the international community to remain steadfast in supporting the democratic process in Haiti.

E. The Junta's Last Gasp: 1988-1990

New elections were held by the CNG on January 17, 1988. Seven of the presidential candidates from November, including frontrunners Marc Bazin, Louis Dejoie, Gerard Gourge and Sylvio Claude, boycotted the elections and voter turnout was reportedly below 5 percent. Moreover, widespread voting irregularities were observed on election day. Leslie Manigat, who had briefly held a cabinet position under François Duvalier and had only recently returned from a long political exile, emerged as the winner. He was widely expected to be a figurehead; his election did not persuade the United States to release the $79 million in annual aid that had been suspended in November 1987.

During the four months following Manigat's inauguration, there were no signs that a change in the regime had taken place. Manigat's promises of eliminating corruption within the bureaucracy and gaining control of the profitable contraband trade appeared rhetorical. However, in June, Manigat, sensing a split within the *junta*, removed Namphy as head of the army and placed him under house arrest. Manigat's ascent proved short-lived. Within 24 hours, the presidential guard freed Namphy, and Manigat was on his way into exile. Namphy declared himself president and assembled a 12-member government that featured only one civilian. In July, Namphy suspended the 1987 Constitution.

On September 17, General Namphy was overthrown by the Haitian army's rank-and-file. The revolt followed the massacre of nine people attending mass at St. Jean Bosco church in Port-au-Prince, the parish of dissident priest Jean-Bertrand Aristide. General Prosper Avril, who emerged as Haiti's new president, immediately dismissed eight generals, including Williams Régala.

Avril promised that his regime would initiate a transition to civilian rule in Haiti. On March 13, 1989, he partially restored the 1987 Constitution. The following month, Avril survived a coup attempt engineered by members of the army's Dessalines Battalion and the elite Leopards Corps. In June, the U.S. Congress, in recognition of Avril's efforts toward restoring constitutional government, authorized $12 million in food aid for Haiti; two months later, USAID released $10 million in aid.

By November 1989, Avril's government still had not announced a timetable for national elections and had begun to suppress political opposition through a series of arrests. An electoral calendar finally published in early January 1990 was negatively received by the political parties and the general public alike. It prescribed a long and elaborate electoral process in which national elections would be held only after elections for local officials. It also failed to restore Article 291 of the 1987 Constitution, thus potentially permitting the candidacies of individuals associated with the Duvalier regime.

On January 20, following the arrest and subsequent deportation of a number of opposition leaders, Avril declared a state of siege. Within 10 days, due to national and international pressures, the state of siege was lifted and Avril declared a "general amnesty" for all political prisoners.

On March 5, at a demonstration in Petit Goâve, an 11-year-old girl was killed by a stray bullet fired by the army. This event provoked a series of student demonstrations around the country. On

March 10, Avril announced his resignation; two days later, a U.S. military aircraft took him to exile in Miami.

A week earlier, the "Group of Twelve," an assembly representing Haiti's 11 major political parties and one civic organization, had called for Avril's resignation. It proposed a provisional government to be led by a member of the Supreme Court and a 19-member Council of State, which would include representatives of 11 different sectors of Haitian society and eight provincial delegates. Thus, on March 13, 1990, Ertha Pascal Trouillot, a Supreme Court judge, assumed the provisional presidency. Her government's sole objective would be to lead the country to free and fair national elections. Trouillot made it clear from the beginning that she had no desire to remain in office beyond the elections.

Chapter 3

ELECTORAL FRAMEWORK

A. Haiti's Political Structure

Immediately upon assuming office, the Trouillot provisional government restored the 1987 Constitution as the fundamental law of Haiti. The constitution establishes Haiti as a republic consisting of nine departments. Each department is divided into communes, which in turn comprise communal sections, the smallest administrative units. Each commune is governed by a three-member municipal council whose president, the mayor, holds a mandate of four years. Each communal section is governed by a three-member administrative council (CASEC), which is elected for four years.

The 1987 Constitution is a hybrid of the French and American models. The president, who is elected for a five-year term, chooses a prime minister to form a government. The parliament consists of two houses, a Chamber of Deputies and a Senate. One deputy is elected from each of Haiti's 83 electoral districts to serve a four-year term. Senators — three from each department — are elected for a six-year period. Senate membership is renewed every two years, with one-third of the seats up for re-election each time.

B. The 1990 Election Law

Before initiating the electoral process, the Trouillot government had to settle the legal status of the most recent Provisional Electoral Council (CEP) appointed by General Avril. In May 1990, the government decided to appoint a new CEP. As stipulated in the 1987 Constitution, the members of the CEP were drawn from nine different sectors of Haitian society. Some of the members were veterans of the first CEP, which organized the aborted 1987 elections, while others had little previous experience with elections.

On July 10, the CEP published a new election law, modeled after the 1987 statute. It provided for the election of all national and local offices on the same day. Candidates in the national races — president of the republic, senators and deputies — needed to win an absolute majority (50 percent + 1) of the votes to gain election. Contests in which none of the candidates obtained a majority of the votes would be decided in run-off elections between the two top vote-getters.

The senators with the highest number of votes in their respective departments would serve six-year terms, while second- and third-place finishers would be elected for four and two years, respectively. Election of the local offices — municipal councils and CASECs — would be decided on the basis of a majority of the votes.

C. The CEP

With the publication of the election law, the CEP could begin organizing for the elections. Its first task was to set up a national CEP structure. By mid-August, the CEP had established its departmental and communal offices (BEDs and BECs). A far greater challenge was hiring and training workers to staff the several thousand registration sites (BIVs). At the same time, the CEP initiated a nationwide voter education program. Following the registration period, the CEP organized the time-consuming task of computerizing and distributing the voter lists and determining the final list of candidates for each office. Finally, the CEP was responsible for printing the ballots.

The cost of the elections (estimated at $12.9 million) proved to be a considerable obstacle to keeping the electoral process on schedule, as the Haitian government found itself unable to finance the entire effort. Accordingly, the electoral calendar had to be modified several times. Finally, registration was scheduled to begin October 5, thus moving the election date to December 16.

A multinational assistance effort, coordinated in part by the UN General Assembly, brought contributions from the United States ($2 million), Canada (materials), Germany (printing costs), France (ballot paper, civic education), and Venezuela (fuel). Other significant contributions were made by Italy and Taiwan.

D. Voter Registration

The official registration period was scheduled for 22 consecutive days, but was then extended by several days to accommodate a late surge of registrants. All Haitians 18 or older on December 16 were eligible to register at a BIV in their neighborhood. The election law stipulated that each BIV was responsible for registering 250 voters. However, due to a shortage of funds, the CEP was unable to hire enough election workers to staff the BIVs and instead made each BIV responsible for compiling several electoral registers. For the elections themselves, additional workers were hired and trained in the requisite number of BIVs.

In order to register to vote, a citizen had to produce one valid piece of identification or present two witnesses who could confirm his or her identity. The registrant's name was then entered into a ledger. Upon registering, each prospective voter received a registration card that he or she would be asked to present on election day as proof of identity and eligibility to vote. Crucial among the information included on the card was the BIV number to which the voter was assigned on election day. Taking into account the high proportion of illiterate voters, the CEP sought to ensure that most Haitians would return on election day to the site at which they had been registered.

Registration proceeded slowly at first, until presidential aspirants began announcing their candidacies. For example, CEP reports suggest that within 48 hours after Father Aristide announced his candidacy, the number of registered voters in the slum neighborhoods of Port-au-Prince and other poor regions of the country doubled. By the end of the registration period, more than 3.2 million Haitians had registered.

The number of voters registered at the national or departmental levels exceeded the estimated number of citizens of voting age. This may be due in part from an underestimation of the figures used in calculating the voting population, as the last population statistics date back to 1982. The social and political events that have taken place since then have altered considerably the base figures.

Throughout the registration period, there were reports alleging instances of double registration. Some of these accusations were verified, and the CEP took the necessary steps to arrest the perpetrators. There was no credible evidence that massive double registration took place. The reasons for some of these irregularities may stem from the nature of the civil registration and personal identification systems in Haiti. It is clear that these systems are in need of modernization, and that permanent electoral rolls must be established to ensure the smooth conduct of future elections.

E. Candidates

New among the provisions of the 1990 election law was the requirement that each candidate pay an election deposit. Fees ranged from 75 *gourdes* ($15) for a member of the CASEC to 4,000 *gourdes* ($800) for a presidential candidate. In addition, each candidate had to submit extensive documentation, including proof of his nomination by a political party or a petition containing signatures in support of his candidacy. An independent presidential candidate, for example, was required to submit 5,000 signatures, with a minimum of 200 from each department.

Much controversy was provoked by the question of how strictly Article 291 of the constitution, which barred certain categories of individuals associated with the former Duvalier regime from holding public office for a period of 10 years, should be applied. This controversy was heightened when Roger Lafontant, the former interior minister and leader of the *tontons macoutes*, reported his intention to enter the presidential race, even though he had been charged with high treason. There was immediate speculation that if excluded, Lafontant would seek revenge by disrupting the elections, thus adding to the pre-election tension.

Lafontant filed his candidacy papers with the Provisional Electoral Council, but made it clear that he considered the body to be illegitimate. Ultimately, the CEP avoided the issue of Duvalierism in Lafontant's case, instead disqualifying him on technical grounds. He had not submitted a valid birth certificate nor had he produced a "certificate of discharge" proving that all government funds had been accounted for when he left the interior ministry in 1985. Meanwhile, the warrant for Lafontant's arrest had become a political football for the Trouillot government. General Abraham, head of the armed forces, requested clarification as to the legality of the warrant, and the matter was referred to the Supreme Court for review, but no action was taken prior to the elections. As time ran out on his legal battle, Lafontant threatened to disrupt the elections.

Leslie Manigat, an academic who had been elected president in the controversial 1988 elections and removed from office five months later by General Henri Namphy, also sought to participate in the 1990 contest. But the provisional government feared that if he returned to Haiti he would reassert his claim to the presidency. Citing *raison d'état*, the Trouillot government instructed all airline carriers serving the country to bar Manigat as a passenger.

Manigat, living in exile in the United States, meanwhile refused to renounce his claim to the presidency. Instead, he announced that he wished to participate in the elections like any other candidate. The Haitian government finally acceded to Manigat's appeal. Upon his return to Haiti, Manigat, known for his prodigious energy, immediately embarked on a non-stop round of press conferences and campaign rallies.

In November, the CEP disqualified Manigat from the race. Its ruling cited Article 134-3 of the 1987 Constitution, which states that "the President of the Republic may not be reelected. He must wait for a five-year interval before running for a second term." According to the CEP's interpretation, Manigat had been elected president in 1988 and, regardless of the circumstances under which he was removed from office, could therefore seek another presidential term only after the prescribed interval had ended. This line of reasoning appeared to leave the CEP vulnerable: if the 1988 elections were valid for the purpose of disqualifying Manigat, why were they invalid for establishing Manigat's claim to be Haiti's legitimate president?

Reacting to the CEP's decision, Manigat argued that the CEP had, in fact, confirmed his status as president of the republic, an office he had never resigned. Nonetheless, contrary to the logic of his claim, Manigat promised to pursue his candidacy, and said that he would simultaneously appeal through the courts to have the CEP decision declared unconstitutional.

The tactic of taking the matter to court, which many contended was a Duvalierist bastion without jurisdiction over the election law, further complicated matters. In the weeks before the elections, the judges heard lawyers from both sides. There were fears that the court, under pressure from the Duvalierists, would somehow cancel the elections. But just before the election, President Trouillot retired two of the judges on the Supreme Court, and the court made no decision on Manigat's case.

F. Printing of the Ballots

Unlike 1987, when separate ballots were printed for each candidate, in 1990 ballots were printed containing the names of all of the candidates for a particular office. (See Appendix XII.) A colored stripe on the back of each ballot matched the color of the ballot box for each of the offices under contention. On the front of each ballot were photographs of the candidates and their respective party symbols. The CEP briefly contemplated not including photographs on the ballot, forcing voters instead to rely on the party symbols to make their choices. This idea was abandoned when party leaders complained that during the entire campaign they had concentrated on personal appearances and picture posters, not abstract party symbols.

Chapter 4

ELECTORAL ENVIRONMENT

A. Parties and Presidential Candidates

Haiti's political parties are in their early stages of development and are, in large measure, personality based. In preparing for the 1990 campaign, the parties were hard pressed to define and articulate comprehensive programs of government. In early November, the CEP narrowed the field of presidential hopefuls to 11 candidates with vastly varying bases of popular support, and whose views covered a broad ideological spectrum. In the pre-election period, it would have been unwise to speculate which of the presidential candidates would emerge as Haiti's next chief executive. Without question however, the real surprise in the race was Father Jean-Bertrand Aristide. The Catholic priest, who drew larger and more enthusiastic crowds than any of his rivals, rode a tidal wave of popular support to the presidential palace through his message of "social justice."

1. Jean-Bertrand Aristide

Since Duvalier's departure in 1986, Father Jean-Bertrand Aristide has been an important political figure in Haiti. From his Port-au-Prince base, he directed a school and a job training program for impoverished youth, and spoke out frequently against the Duvalierist *macoute* forces. Aristide was instrumental in organizing opposition to the successive military-led regimes since 1987, and was the target of several assassination attempts. His critics included the traditional Catholic church hierarchy, which ultimately proscribed him from performing parish duties as a consequence of his political activities; the most affluent members of Haitian society, who feared his radical theology and its call for redistribution of wealth in the country; and conservative elements of the armed forces, who were worried about his ability to mobilize the masses with an uncompromising message calling for social transformation.

In the pre-election period, Aristide opposed elections "at any cost." In interviews at home and abroad he declared that it would not be possible to hold free elections in a climate of insecurity. In Aristide's view, those responsible for the 1987 election-related violence would have to be brought to justice before the process could move forward. As for his own role, Father Aristide denied that he harbored presidential ambitions, saying "I don't suffer from that sickness." Despite his strong following, Aristide was seen by many as someone outside or even above the political game.

Nonetheless, in late October, Aristide became the presidential candidate of the National Front for Democratic Convergence (FNCD). The FNCD, whose leadership was drawn largely from the radical clergy, initially had opposed elections. The FNCD leaders espoused "social justice," which some interpreted as a campaign of revenge against remnants of the Duvalierist era. Aristide, at first, explained his candidacy as a response to the candidacy of Lafontant. However, having entered the contest, he never seemed to consider withdrawing, even when Lafontant's candidacy was rejected.

Aristide's campaign, which he called *lavalas*, or cleansing flood, sought to rise above the old order and promote a new society based on "justice for the disenfranchised." Aristide was renowned for his simple yet moving sermons, and his translation of proverbs and symbols of Haitian folk culture into prescriptions for political action. During campaign appearances attended by record crowds, Aristide struck a chord of solidarity with the victims of political violence and encouraged voters to overcome their fears by joining *lavalas*. "With many hands, the burden is light," he preached. Aristide was confident of victory from the very beginning of his campaign.

2. *Marc Bazin*

Prior to 1986, Marc Bazin worked as a World Bank official and served briefly as a minister of finance under Jean-Claude Duvalier, where he waged an honorable, but ultimately unsuccessful, campaign against corruption. Bazin returned to Haiti in 1986 to found the Movement for the Installation of Democracy in Haiti (MIDH). For the 1990 elections, the MIDH joined forces with Serge Gilles' Socialist PANPRA party and Déjean Belizaire's MNP-28. This tripartite alliance, which became known as the National Alliance for Democracy and Progress (ANDP), chose Bazin as its presidential candidate.

With other politicians wavering in their support for elections, even after Trouillot assumed office, Bazin was committed to participation. He believed that even if the current climate was less than ideal, there had been a fundamental shift from the situation in 1987; this time, the government and the army were committed to the process. "If you want to get out of a situation of political chaos, institutional disorder and poverty, there must be a government with popular legitimacy which is based on the exercise of national sovereignty by means of elections," Bazin said.

Bazin, based on his experience in international finance, promised that, if elected, he would be able to obtain substantial aid and investment from abroad to rebuild the Haitian economy. His program called for the promotion of Haitian exports and greater integration of Haiti into the U.S. market. Protectionist legislation, he argued, isolated Haiti within the region. Finally, Bazin stressed the need to eliminate the corrupt vestiges of Duvalierism in the public sector, while building an efficient infrastructure for the economy.

3. *Other candidates*

Louis Déjoie, Jr., ran on a populist platform as leader of the National Party for Agriculture and Industry (PAIN). Déjoie inherited a loyal following in the southern region of the country from his father, who had opposed François Duvalier in the controversial 1957 elections. As the rift between the provisional government and the Council of State widened in late summer, Déjoie joined left-of-center organizations and refused to support the election process. Once voter registration began, however, Déjoie launched a vigorous presidential campaign. Although PAIN's progressive platform was similar in some respects to that of Aristide's FNCD, Déjoie hoped that his establishment credentials would prove persuasive to centrist voters.

Reverend Sylvio Claude was the candidate of the Christian Democratic Party of Haiti (PDCH). Like most of its rivals, the PDCH had a weak organization; however, it was buoyed by its leader's fiery personality. A former taxi driver, Claude was a colorful orator who had been arrested and tortured during the Duvalier era. His campaign slogan, "Here is the martyr," stressed his sacrifice. With his base in the Protestant community and a national reputation as a result of his years in the opposition, Claude was considered a strong candidate before Aristide entered the race. Convinced that 1990 would be his year of triumph, Claude rejected the calls from other parties to delay the election process. Aristide's late entry into the race cut deeply into Claude's base and attracted many of the undecided who were waiting for a "people's candidate" to break out of the pack. As his support eroded, Claude denounced Aristide as a "communist."

Thomas Desulmé was the candidate of the National Labor Party (PNT). Although he joined the race late, Desulmé was the candidate with the longest political history. A former member of parliament, in the 1950s he was a young adherent of the *noiriste* philosophy, which recognized Haiti's African cultural roots and promoted the emerging black middle class. Desulmé managed François Duvalier's 1957 presidential campaign, but went into exile a year later. Desulmé launched successful factories in Jamaica and later returned to invest in the new Port-au-Prince assembly plants. Desulmé hoped to position his center-right party as an alternative to Bazin.

Hubert De Ronceray was the candidate of the National Movement for Democracy (MDN). A social scientist who had served briefly as a cabinet member under Jean-Claude Duvalier, De Ronceray appealed to conservatives and concentrated his campaign around his base in Petit Goave in the Western Department.

René Théodore, candidate of the Haitian Communist Party (PUCH), was Aristide's harshest critic on the left. His accusations that Aristide may have had prior knowledge of the St. Jean Bosco massacre backfired on the campaign trail and undermined his base of support.

Volvick Rémy Joseph, candidate of the Movement for National Cooperation (MKN), was an avowed Duvalierist, although not tainted by any personal role in "zealous excesses" proscribed by the 1987 Constitution. He contrasted the relative prosperity under the former regime to the current state of decay, and appealed for support from all Haitians, including the *macoutes*.

B. The Election Campaign

In early September, the electoral process was given impetus by the promulgation of the election law, announcement of the election calendar and promises of international support. The election campaign officially began on November 7, and although security concerns remained, political parties launched their first rallies. The CEP had approved the candidacies of 11 presidential candidates, 131 for the Senate and 382 for the Chamber of Deputies.

The first and the most ambitious rally was the ANDP's inaugural rally in St. Marc, Bazin's birthplace. The media estimated attendance between 5,000 and 7,000 and, echoing Aristide's allegation of "dollar rallies," charged that the cost of producing such an event showed that the ANDP would spend any amount to defeat its rivals. The ANDP tried to turn this image to its advantage, saying it proved not only that Bazin could raise money for a campaign but also that he would be able to attract investment to Haiti's economy once elected.

As the campaign progressed, the gap widened between a well-honed ANDP campaign machine, rich in talent and resources, and that same campaign's inability to muster large-scale popular support. The ANDP followed a two-tiered strategy of cultivating influential local leaders, who in the past could be relied upon to motivate their followers, and of making contact with key representative sectors in Haitian society.

The campaigns of other candidates followed the conventional course of public meetings, press conferences and weekend campaign rallies. Although police protection for candidates was limited, there were no complaints, and the early campaign was not marred by serious incidents. Party funds were scarce, and the logistical challenges of bad roads and unreliable communications hampered the activities of all candidates.

The Haitian election campaign was transformed in late October, when Roger Lafontant and Father Jean-Bertrand Aristide entered the race as presidential candidates. Within 48 hours of Aristide's announcement, voter registration reportedly doubled in many regions of the country. While the number of inscriptions had been steadily increasing for weeks, this last-minute surge forced the CEP to extend the sign-up period by a few days. Aristide's advisers were convinced that the priest would be able to draw on a sizeable reservoir of support from undecided voters and from those who so far had felt excluded from the process.

While it may have appeared that his movement had formed overnight, Aristide was in fact supported by an effective national network. The *ti legliz* or little church, which represented a Haitian version of liberation theology, stationed energetic priests throughout the country who could mobilize the people for their candidate. Some observers thought that Aristide's supporters were either too young to vote, or that they joined the campaign too late to register. There was concern among all the parties that first-time and illiterate voters would have difficulty casting valid ballots. Acknowledging these potential obstacles, the FNCD mounted an effort to educate their supporters on how to vote and emphasized the FNCD's symbol, the rooster.

C. Campaign Issues

While Aristide spoke of his love for the poor and promised to lift Haiti "from misery and poverty," he avoided presenting a detailed description of his program of government. Peasant land reformers contended with Marxist theorists and successful businessmen within the FNCD to shape the program. Aristide played down the internal divisions and declared that a vibrant business community was essential to development.

Justice was a key issue during the campaign. Bazin advocated evolutionary change through democratic government, not a radical restructuring of institutions or a "rooting out" of individuals suspected of past abuses. Aristide espoused a vision of a Haiti once and for all freed from the domination of the Duvalierists and their *macoute* henchmen. Although Aristide denied charges that he favored "people's tribunals" to deal with *macoute* criminals, some wealthy Haitians and others who were not Duvaliersts but had prospered under the former regime, feared a wholesale settling of accounts outside of the law if Aristide were to be elected. Perhaps to disarm his critics and broaden his base, Aristide later toned down his rhetoric, and spoke of Haitian soldiers as "sons of the people" who deserved to be held in esteem for doing their duty. He encouraged the support of "honest, democratic officers."

As a result of his contacts in the United States, Bazin was perceived by many as the "American candidate." In Aristide's case, on the other hand, there was concern, based on his past criticism of U.S. policy toward Haiti, that, if elected, he would alienate the U.S. government. During the campaign, Aristide emphasized that Haiti and the United States should stand as equals and negotiate openly, "without flattery or humiliation." This message helped change Aristide's image somewhat from that of an outside activist to one of a candidate prepared to assume the responsibilities of a head of state.

D. Media Coverage of the Campaign

After the fall of Jean-Claude Duvalier, a new generation of Haitian journalists, untainted by past associations, emerged. While the limits on freedom of the press varied under the military-led governments, an expansion of media outlets, notably radio stations, helped the press change from an official vehicle to a forum for the Creole- and French-speaking public. Under the provisional government, journalists reported on current affairs with little restraint.

The Haitian media demonstrated a strong institutional commitment to covering all facets of the electoral process. Every political party and tendency found expression in the media; interviews and press releases, often unabridged, were freely disseminated. Some critics charged that the press was overly sympathetic to Aristide, but overall, the coverage was open enough to allow voters to evaluate the candidates and make informed judgements.

The national television station, TNH, was perhaps the most neutral medium for election coverage. The evening news broadcast and public affairs programs provided reasonably equal coverage to the candidates. The presidential contenders, however, never accepted the offer to participate in a televised debate.

Both the print media and television had limited reach outside of the capital. The majority of Haitians followed the campaign by listening to local radio stations.

E. Security Concerns

1. Hotel Santos

By June, the 19-member Council of State, the quasi-legislative body comprising representatives from different sectors of Haitian society, and provisional President Trouillot had ceased to cooperate in the spirit of the March 4, 1990 accord. The Council alleged that Trouillot had failed to exert civilian control over the armed forces, that political violence was flourishing and that the government was withholding financial data. The latter dispute focused on Trouillot's appointment of Violène Legagneur, said to be a founding member of a Duvalierist political party, to the post of finance minister. Increased street violence exacerbated the stand off. During the third week of June, 13 people were killed during a 48-hour period in Port-au-Prince.

On June 21, the Council of State organized a meeting with representatives of trade unions and grassroots organizations to discuss solutions to the political crisis. The meeting, held at the Hotel Santos in Port-au-Prince, was disrupted when four armed men, two in army uniforms and two in civilian garb, entered the lobby and opened fire with automatic rifles. Jean-Marie Montés, a union leader, was killed instantly. Emmanuel Mani, member of the Socialist National

Progressive Party, and Serge Villard, a member of the Council, were wounded. Villard later died of his injuries.

Council members who witnessed the shooting said that policemen guarding a government building in front of the hotel made no effort to prevent the killers' escape. They further charged that when soldiers arrived later, they neglected to collect evidence such as shell casings, failed to interview witnesses and did not offer protection to the surviving members of the Council. The attack reinforced the lack of trust between the Council of State and the government. It also heightened concerns about election security.

To meet these mounting concerns, General Abraham formed a Security Coordinating Committee (SCC), whose members were colonels representing critical elements of the armed forces. The SCC was charged by Abraham with drafting a national plan for election security, and did so in consultation with UN security advisors. The group proposed a series of emergency measures to help guarantee a secure election environment.

In carrying out the plan, military departmental commanders were granted broad discretionary authority in the conduct of their operations. Though the security plan was nationwide in scope, priority was given to the Port-au-Prince metropolitan area, and troops were instructed to respect the election law, to refrain from the use of arms, to remain impartial and to cooperate fully with civilian CEP personnel and the voters at large. The departmental commanders, whose resources were extremely limited, were required to redeploy some of their personnel assets. The military commanders coordinated their efforts with the CEP, and this high level of cooperation was crucial to the overall success of the election security program.

2. Lafontant's return and candidacy

In July, when Roger Lafontant returned to Haiti, it was widely believed that his true objective was to seize upon the provisional government's perceived weakness and mount a *coup d'état*. While the government's chief prosecutor issued a warrant for Lafontant's arrest on charges of high treason, his supporters took to the streets of the capital threatening motorists and chanting "Long live Lafontant!"

The refusal of police authorities to execute the warrant and the unchecked acts of intimidation further polarized Haitian society.

Lafontant's return coincided with increased violence, which Haitians described as the campaign of "insecurity." In the capital, there was an outbreak of murders and violent assaults. The perpetrators were believed to be off-duty soldiers or hoodlums, known as *zinglendos*. Although the victims of *zinglendo* attacks seldom seemed to have been singled out for overt political reasons, the violence raised the level of anxiety concerning election security. The nightly violence conveyed the message that Lafontant was determined to leave his mark on the elections. In Gonaives, the CEP's offices were attacked. Excrement and graffiti smeared on the walls, "Down with Article 291," identified those who were responsible. Later, when burgeoning voter registration levels showed a public largely in support of the elections, Lafontant shifted gears and decided to run for president. His new party, the National Union for Reconciliation (UNR), comprised hard-core Duvalierists.

Soon after Lafontant's return, labor organizations and left-of-center political parties launched a general strike to highlight their demand for Trouillot's resignation if the order to arrest Lafontant was not carried out. In a rare public statement, Trouillot appealed for unity and denounced demagogues who might try to prevent elections through violence or "crooked wheeling-dealing." In August, the Council of State announced a "complete break" with the embattled chief executive. The Council claimed that it had exhausted all avenues of negotiation and concluded that Trouillot was an "obstacle in the path of genuine elections." As political malaise ensued, gasoline shortages and frequent blackouts darkened the mood within the country.

Lafontant's candidacy, announced in mid-October, raised the stakes for the government and challenged the CEP's authority. If he were disqualified on the basis of Article 291 of the constitution, Lafontant warned, it would mean the repudiation of an entire class of Haitians who sought nothing more than to exercise their right to political expression. Ironically, however, the most direct result of Lafontant's electoral stratagem was to create the conditions for

Aristide's move to abandon his role as outside critic and enter the race with the avowed mission of stopping Lafontant's bid for power.

A consensus slowly emerged that elections offered the only way out of the morass. Promises of foreign financial support for the election process helped inspire confidence. As electoral activity increased, Trouillot became more visible in her role as head of state. While the provisional government never enjoyed wide popular support, its image improved as the reality of the elections drew near.

3. Pétionville massacre

Election violence erupted on December 5 at an Aristide rally in the heart of Pétionville, a wealthy suburb north of the capital. At the time, there was some expectation among the public that the Supreme Court, in the next day or two, would declare the CEP illegal. For his part, Aristide exhorted his supporters to mobilize "people power" to resist any attempts to derail the elections.

After Aristide finished speaking, the electrical power was cut and thousands were left in darkness. Two men jumped out of a jeep; one man hurled a fragmentation grenade at the group of pedestrians while the other raked the crowd with machine gun fire. Seven people were killed; some 50 more were severely hurt by the bomb blast.

The morning after the bloodshed, the army announced the formation of a committee to investigate the attack and solicited leads from the public. Several arrests, including some of Lafontant's bodyguards, were reportedly made prior to the elections. The minister of the interior issued a pronouncement forbidding all demonstrations by "populist" groups. In order to hold rallies, presidential candidates needed to seek the army's permission 48 hours in advance. This order effectively terminated the public campaign period. Schools were closed until after the elections.

The Pétionville massacre, however, did not diminish the public's commitment to the elections. During the days that followed, all presidential candidates condemned the attack and pledged to uphold the election law. The Pétionville incident, for which Lafontant was widely suspected of being responsible, underscored the importance of the election security plan. Drafted by the army in coordination with the CEP and UN security advisors, the strategy called for a nationwide deployment of troops, traffic restrictions and protection of polling sites.

Chapter 5

ELECTION DAY

This chapter describes activities on December 16, election day. It includes specific observations regarding the voting process compiled from the reports of the Council/NDI teams stationed in Port-au-Prince and around the country.

A. Balloting Process

In order to vote, Haitians had been instructed to return to the same election offices (BIVs) where they had registered two months earlier. The number and location of the BIV were indicated on each voter's registration card. A total of approximately 14,000 BIVs were established around the country, each serving 250 registered voters. Frequently, these BIVs were located in schools, churches or other centers that were able to house a number of polling sites in a single building.

A staff of three, sometimes four, election officials — president, secretary and one or two clerks — were hired by the CEP to administer the vote at each BIV. At many BIVs, security was provided by an armed military guard posted outside the door. In accordance with the Haitian electoral law, representatives of the political parties were admitted inside the BIVs to observe the voting. In addition, the CEP accredited more than 1,000 international observers, among them the members of the Council/NDI delegation. On election day, Haitians were asked to choose: a president of the republic from among 11 approved candidates; 27 senators from among 119 approved candidates; 83 deputies from among 337 approved candidates; 135 three-member municipal councils from among 534 approved ones; and 565 three-member administrative councils of the communal sections (CASECs) from among 1,539 approved ones.

The polls were scheduled to open at 6 a.m. By that time on election day, many Haitians had already arrived and were lined up outside the BIVs. Early reports from the provinces indicated that the polls were opening within an hour or so of the scheduled time. In and around Port-au-Prince, however, the late delivery of ballot boxes and other materials forced a delay of two hours or more at many polling sites. By 8 a.m., the elections were underway in most areas of the capital, a significant exception being the slum neighborhood of Cité Soleil, which did not receive its materials until 2 p.m.

Upon entering the BIV, each voter was asked to present his or her voter identification card. The voter's name was then checked off the list of registered voters. The CEP was supposed to have distributed these registers in the form of computer printouts; however, many of the BIVs were forced to rely on the original handwritten ledgers that had been compiled during the registration period.

Having been identified as a registered voter, each voter was given ballots for the national and local elections. Voters were then shown to a corner of the BIV where one or more *isoloirs* (cardboard screens, approximately two-feet high) had been set up to ensure privacy. Voters indicated their choice by making a mark inside the circle beneath their candidate's photograph. After placing the ballots in the appropriate color-coded ballot boxes, an election official dipped the voter's thumb in indelible ink to indicate that the person had voted.

Despite inexperience with the prescribed procedures, voting in most areas proceeded smoothly; by noon, it appeared that between 40 and 50 percent of the votes had been cast. It should be noted that in many cases BIVs did not receive ballots for the election of the municipal councils or the Administrative Councils of the Communal Sections (CASECs). A series of "make-up" elections was held for these offices throughout January 1991.

During the day, with a few exceptions, the atmosphere at the polls was generally one of enthusiasm and anticipation, as Haitians waited peacefully and patiently for their chance to vote for the first time in free and democratic elections. Because of the limited organizational structure of Haiti's political parties, none of them could place representatives at all of the BIVs throughout the country. Only Jean-Bertrand Aristide's FNCD was consistently represented. The other major presidential contender, Marc Bazin, whose ANDP had tried during the campaign to distinguish itself as Haiti's only political party with a truly national organization, was also strongly represented, but far less than had been anticipated. Nonetheless, every effort was made to administer the voting process as openly as possible. The response by the Haitian voters, election officials and party pollwatchers to the presence of the international observers was universally positive.

Prior to election day, the greatest concern regarding the elections had been the security of voters and election officials. It was generally expected that Lafontant, who had been disqualified from participating in the presidential race, would retaliate by ordering his men to disrupt the elections through violent means. There was a question as to whether Haiti's small army, which had been implicated in the 1987 election-day violence, would be able to guarantee security at the polls. As it happened, the day passed without incident. The army controlled roads and posted armed guards near all of the major polling sites. Further, the army, with the assistance of UN security advisors and observers, who by their presence, helped to reassure the population and encourage the dialogue between the civil authorities, regained the confidence of the Haitian people.

During election day, the CEP was preoccupied by the problems stemming from the failure to deliver election materials to certain polling sites, particularly those in the poor sections of the capital. President Carter visited the CEP mid-morning on election day to report the delegation's initial observation of problems in certain areas. It became obvious at the time that the CEP was hampered by its lack of a nationwide communications network, and so was not in a position to evaluate the magnitude of the problems nor to respond effectively to the problems.

In the early afternoon, President Carter and several members of the delegation returned to CEP headquarters. A meeting between CEP officials and representatives of the political parties was underway. The CEP estimated that approximately 1,000 polling stations (out of 14,000) had not opened on time. In view of this situation, several of the political party leaders recommended that voting be extended, perhaps for a day, in those places where materials were not available, while others suggested that the voting resume the following week. The CEP was concerned that extending the polling would cause additional problems, given the already prescribed procedures.

Eventually, reports from the UN and other observers convinced the CEP that the problems were localized in certain areas and that by 1 p.m. virtually all sites had become operational. President Carter and others then urged the CEP to extend the polling for several hours to permit all those desiring to vote an opportunity to do so. As the meeting between CEP officials and party leaders became more heated, President Carter telephoned General Abraham to seek his approval for the extension of the voting hours. Abraham deferred to the minister of justice, who ruled that the CEP could not legally extend hours of voting.

Leaving the CEP building, President Carter held an impromptu press conference at which time he asked the radio and television stations to announce that, in accordance with the law, the polling stations would remain open until all those in line were permitted to vote. In this way, Carter sought to encourage those individuals who had left the polling sites in frustration to return and cast their ballots, while alleviating tension among those who viewed the failure to deliver materials as part of a conspiracy designed to hurt Aristide's candidacy.

B. Specific Observations

The delegation witnessed administrative irregularities at a number of polling sites. On the whole, however, these may safely be attributed to the lack of experience on the part of both voters and election officials. Working long hours without meals and having to compensate for a lack of resources, officials at the BIVs were frequently forced to improvise and did so successfully, ensuring that the balloting proceeded smoothly. Logistical failures, though especially significant in the case of Cité Soleil, had been expected, considering the difficulty and unprecedented nature of the CEP's undertaking. But, as one delegation member put it, "there was no sign of manipulation, just inefficiency."

1. Voter identification

In verifying that a voter had been properly registered at a particular BIV, election officials were occasionally handicapped by a lack of materials and changes in the BIV's structure. For example, BIVs that had registered 500 voters were subsequently divided to meet the 250 voter limit, though they generally continued to operate in the same room. In some of these cases, the BIVs set up adjacent tables and shared voter lists. However, at a polling site in Carrefour, a suburb of Port-au-Prince, two such BIVs had set up their tables on opposite sides of the room; thus, since only one handwritten ledger of registered voters was available, one of the BIVs was forced to admit voters solely based on the presentation of voter identification cards.

2. Ballot secrecy

Several observer teams witnessed election officials providing assistance to voters who had difficulty marking their ballots. In the town of Jérémie, election officials were observed actually filling out ballots for older and disabled voters. In Carrefour and in the southern port city of Les Cayes, party pollwatchers in a few cases assisted voters directly or stood over them as they marked their ballots.

A number of factors made violations of voter privacy almost inevitable: 1) the novelty of the exercise for voters and officials alike; 2) the high level of illiteracy among the voters; 3) the claustrophobic nature of most BIVs that made it virtually impossible for voters to isolate themselves completely; and 4) the eagerness of election officials (and party pollwatchers) to assist confused voters. However, there did not appear to be an effort on the part of any party to intimidate voters or manipulate voter inexperience to their advantage. Based on these observations, the delegation concluded that the practice of assisting voters was local and exceptional rather than nationally directed.

3. Delivery of election materials

In the case of Cité Soleil, the slum neighborhood of Port-au-Prince that was an Aristide stronghold, the CEP's failure to deliver election materials on time nearly provoked massive unrest that could have jeopardized the entire election process. When by the end of the morning, ballot boxes had still not arrived, Aristide's supporters, convinced that they had been deliberately disenfranchised, began to threaten violence. Finally, at around 2 p.m., the materials arrived, though more than half a day of voting had been lost. Many voters had already returned to their homes, however, and by the time the polls closed, voter lines had disappeared at most of the polling sites.

C. Counting Process

Shortly after 6 p.m., the counting of the ballots began at most BIVs. The only individuals present in the BIVs at this time were election officials, party pollwatchers and international observers. Counting the ballots was a straightforward process: the box with the presidential ballots was opened first, each ballot then taken out and the vote read aloud. That process was then repeated for the other offices. The secretary of the BIV recorded the results of each election on tally sheets. Copies of the tally sheets were prepared and signed by all of the observers present. Everywhere, election officials took great pains to give everyone present a view of each ballot; this slowed the counting of the votes, but left no doubts about the openness of the process.

Once the votes for all the offices were counted, each BIV forwarded two copies of the results to the Departmental Election Office (BED). All ballots and registration lists were also returned to the BED. At the BED, results from all of the BIVs within each department were tabulated. The departmental results were then transmitted to the CEP, which conducted the final tabulation.

The procedures at the BEDs, however, left much to be desired. There was a great deal of confusion as officials brought materials, hastily tied together, and just left them for the officials. In other cases, the procedures for tabulating the results were not being implemented in an efficient manner. Consequently, there were significant delays in tabulating the results at the BEDs and in reporting them to the CEP headquarters.

In this context, the parallel vote tabulation (PVT) undertaken jointly by the UN and OAS proved critical in providing accurate information to the CEP and, then by extension, to the government, the political party leaders and the public. The UN and OAS PVT relied on the presidential results from a random sample of approximately 130 polling stations (less than 1 percent of the total). While there was some concern regarding the small size of the sample, UN and OAS officials designed the PVT with two modest goals in mind: 1) to determine if any presidential candidate had obtained near the 50 percent total necessary to avoid a run-off; and 2) assuming no candidate obtained a majority, to determine which two candidates had obtained the largest number of votes.

To implement the PVT operation, the UN and OAS established a sophisticated radio network that covered the entire country. Moreover, because the organizations pooled their resources, they had sufficient personnel to cover all of the polling sites designated by the sample and avoided the prospect of inconsistent results.

The system worked to perfection. UN and OAS officials in Port-au-Prince began receiving the results from observers in the field as soon as the counting of the presidential ballots at the BIV level was completed. At midnight, the head of the UN and OAS teams visited CEP headquarters to report the results of the PVT, but promised, per a prior agreement with the CEP (and in accordance with the election law), not to release the PVT results publicly.

CEP officials, who had spent a hectic day coping with various administrative problems and were now faced with the reality of delays in the tabulation process, appeared relieved that the PVT had worked effectively. No longer fearing that the release of partial results would be construed as constituting an unfair trending of the results in favor of a particular candidate, the CEP officials promised to release the results the following morning.

In any event, the tabulation process still took longer than anticipated, and it was not until the following afternoon that the first returns were released by the CEP. This small sample of the returns showed Aristide winning by nearly 70 percent of the national vote.

On December 24, eight days after the elections, the CEP finally announced the victory of Jean-Bertrand Aristide. Official results from the first round of the elections were not published until January 14. They showed Aristide winning with 67.5 percent of the vote, followed by Marc Bazin with 14.2 percent. Official tallies also indicated that approximately 63 percent of the eligible voters participated in the December 16 elections.

The results of the presidential elections were immediately accepted by the other 10 contestants and by the international community. Results from the national elections showed that the majority of the seats (22 in the Senate, 42 in the Chamber of Deputies, 33 communes and approximately 140 communal sections) would have to be decided in run-off elections on January 20, 1991.

Chapter 6

ELECTION AFTERMATH

The December 16 general elections in Haiti marked a dramatic turning point, and represented the nation's best hope for a full transition to democracy. Despite fears of election-related violence, the elections were conducted in a generally peaceful and efficient manner. For many Haitians, the sight of soldiers guarding voters and ballot boxes, and working side by side with civilian election officials around the country, was considered miraculous.

By early January 1991, post-election euphoria had dissipated. During a January 1 homily, Port-au-Prince Archbishop Wolff Ligondé, a pro-Duvalier cleric, labeled President-elect Aristide a "socio-Bolshevik" whose intent was to build a dictatorship. The prelate's residence was later sacked and burned to the ground by mobs of Aristide supporters. The mobs also destroyed the Vatican nuncio's residence, the Catholic Bishops' Conference headquarters and a 387-year-old cathedral, which was believed to be the oldest in the Caribbean. Ligondé, the nuncio and other church officials went into hiding. President-elect Aristide expressed regret that symbols of the Roman Catholic Church had been the object of the rampages, but for one week the roving mobs continued seeking revenge against remnants of the Duvalier regime.

A. January 6 Coup Attempt

On the evening of January 6, Lafontant, together with a small group of armed supporters, abducted President Trouillot at her private residence. Bringing Trouillot to the National Palace, they forced her to broadcast a resignation announcement. In the early hours of January 7, Lafontant announced that he had assumed the provisional presidency of Haiti.

Much to Lafontant's surprise, the people of Haiti refused to accept the overthrow of the government, which also would deny President-elect Aristide the office he had won so decisively. The word of Lafontant's action spread immediately throughout Port-au-Prince and the rest of the country. Aristide's outraged supporters took to the streets and demanded that the armed forces move immediately and decisively to defend Haiti's fragile democracy by arresting Lafontant.

By mid-morning on January 7, the army responded by opening fire on the National Palace. Meeting little resistance, the armed forces arrested Lafontant. Trouillot resumed her office as provisional president. Meanwhile, pro-Aristide vigilantes destroyed Lafontant's URN party headquarters, and the party offices and personal property of other political leaders around the country. The violence resulted in the deaths of at least 50 people.

The Lafontant coup attempt and the ensuing violence contributed to an air of apprehension in Haiti, not only regarding the run-off elections, but about the prospects for a peaceful transition to a new government. In the aftermath of the rebellion, and prior to the January 20 run-off elections, there was considerable concern among leaders and ordinary citizens that the democratic process in Haiti might yet be derailed prior to Aristide's February 7 inauguration.

B. Preparations for the January 20 Run-off

In preparation for the January 20 run-off, during which more than half the seats in both houses of parliament and local offices would be decided, the CEP took concrete steps to improve its administration of the elections, particularly in the Western Department. The CEP acquired helicopters to enhance its election-day logistics operation. The Haitian National Federation of Teachers agreed to appoint pollwatchers at each BIV throughout the country to ensure that each polling site would have literate personnel available to assist voters. Although this did not occur everywhere, a credible effort was apparently made by the teachers and the CEP.

Because there were fewer candidates, the run-off ballots were simplified, and most voters were already familiar with the procedures for casting their ballots. The CEP therefore expected fewer problems, and hoped that it would be able to tabulate the ballots more quickly than it had in December. Cooperation between the CEP and the armed forces also continued. Because of the nature of the run-off elections, and the general impression on the part of many voters that the main race had been decided in December, there were predictions that the voter turnout in the run-off would not exceed 50 percent. These predictions proved correct.

C. The Run-off Election

Haitians went to the polls on January 20 to elect members of parliament and local officials in far fewer numbers than on December 16. The CEP's previous public education program in support of the elections was not evident during the run-off and, unlike in December, there was no sense of excitement about the election process among the electorate. This general ambivalence might be attributed to recent acts of violence, but also to a lack of understanding on the part of the voters about the relevance of parliament and the local offices. Further, political party leaders generally released their candidates to decide individually whether they would compete in the elections. Few political party campaign activities took place during the period leading up to the run-off.

OAS and UN observers were once more present, although their delegations were far smaller than in December. Given the fact that few parliamentary and local races were contested in Port-au-Prince, the NDI team travelled to Carrefour, on the outskirts of the capital, where the morning voting was extremely light. The team noted at several polling sites the absence of BIV signs outside the buildings; that some ballot boxes had not been sealed; that there was a marked absence of security personnel; and that BIV officials were generally without computerized voter registration lists. The team later heard of a report from one polling site that an independent candidate for mayor of Carrefour had allegedly bribed BIV workers to stuff their ballot boxes. Police arrested the workers, and the CEP canceled the balloting at that site.

Later in the morning, the team visited Léogane and continued south toward Jacmel, where it witnessed voting in some of Haiti's rural areas. Some BIVs were located in straw huts and wooden cottages, but were operated by young people strongly committed to completing the election process. The level of voter activity was slightly higher in Jacmel, and the armed forces were present at most polling sites there. Returning to Port-au-Prince in the late afternoon, the team met with CEP officials who confirmed that the day's balloting had proceeded without major incident, although some administrative irregularities and logistical problems had been noted.

The final results of the parliamentary elections were not as clear-cut as the presidential race. No single party obtained a majority of the seats in either house of parliament. It should be noted that none of the parties was able to field candidates in all of the parliamentary contests; for example, the FNCD, which now holds the plurality in both houses, could not technically have won a majority of the deputy seats.

In the municipal elections, the FNCD and the ANDP were clearly the dominant political groups, with FNCD candidates winning in a slightly larger number of communes. Aristide's party was especially strong in the Artibonite, the Center Department, and the Western Department. Independent candidates also played significant roles in these races. (See Appendix XIII for a list of final presidential and National Assembly election results.)

For the second time in less than a month, Haitians participated in generally peaceful elections, with the civilian and military elements of the Haitian government cooperating in support of a new democratic era for the country. These positive developments were tempered, however, by the social, economic and political challenges that await the new government.

D. The Inauguration

Despite uneasiness regarding the transition, the inauguration was peaceful and indeed joyous. Tens of thousands of people descended on the capital to celebrate.

Prior to the inauguration, Aristide held a series of meetings with General Abraham, and the two reached an important understanding on the relationship between the new civilian authority and the military as an institution. President Aristide described that new understanding in general terms in his inaugural address, and it augers well for the democratic transition. Although some had feared that Aristide would try to establish a popular militia as a counterweight to the military, he made clear his determination to work with the military under the rule of law. He told his people that during his administration, the military would defend and protect the people, and that they should show their support for the armed forces. He also informed the military that it would be subordinate to civil authorities, and he demonstrated this resolve by retiring many senior officers, but expressed the nation's appreciation for their years of prior service.

To those who were concerned that his new administration might turn inward and try to isolate Haiti from the outside world, President Aristide also underscored his desire to seek cooperation and aid from the entire international community.

Delegation member Andrew Young reviews election security arrangements with Armed Forces Chief of Staff Herard Abraham, October 1990.

Delegation members Denzil Douglas (far left), Andrew Young (center) and Beatrice Rangel discuss international observer coordination with OAS Secretary General Joao Baena Soares (right), October 1990.

Delegation meets with President Ertha Pascal Trouillot prior to elections, December 1990.

Balloting commences in Port-au-Prince, December 1990.

Haitian citizens wait in line to vote in Carrefour, December 1990.

Delegation members Robert McNamara and Robert Pastor witness beginning of voting in Port-au-Prince, December 1990.

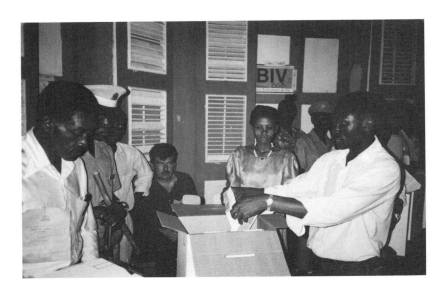

Delegation member Esteban Caballero (seated) observes the vote counting process in Hinche, December 1990.

Observer delegation holds post-election press conference, December 17, 1990. Seated (l to r) are delegation co-leaders: George Price, Jimmy Carter and John Whitehead.

Chapter 7

REFLECTIONS ON THE HAITIAN ELECTORAL PROCESS

The Council/NDI delegation observed the 1990 Haitian elections in accordance with internationally recognized standards for monitoring electoral processes. The delegation's presence, together with observers from the UN, the OAS, CARICOM, the United States, Canada, Venezuela and other countries, demonstrated the international community's unprecedented interest in and support for free elections and democratization in Haiti. It was the Haitian people, however, who judged the significance and validity of these elections, through their participation at the polls and their acceptance of the results.

In contrast to the tragic elections of 1987, the Haitian government in 1990 exhibited a strong commitment to the election process, providing added confidence to the electorate. There were no mixed signals given to the electorate, and the degree of cooperation was exemplary among the different institutions responsible for assuring that the elections were conducted in a free and peaceful manner. President Trouillot, General Abraham and the armed forces, and the Provisional Electoral Council are to be congratulated for their roles during this critical period.

In evaluating the overall election process, the delegation noted that the pre-election campaign period provided the political candidates an opportunity to communicate their respective messages to the public through rallies, the media and other outlets. While there was tension and a great degree of anxiety among the electorate regarding security issues, for the most part, the campaign and the election were conducted in a peaceful manner, although several violent incidents did occur. At most of the polling places visited by the delegation on election day, the process enabled voters to cast their ballots without fear and intimidation. In spite of some irregularities, most Haitians were permitted the chance to participate in these historic elections.

The Haitian elections, while far from perfect, provided an opportunity for a long oppressed people to express themselves through a democratic process, and granted President Jean-Bertrand Aristide a broad popular mandate for democratic change. Still, it is not clear what explains the Aristide phenomenon. Clearly, he identified with the masses and the population's desire to break sharply with the past. There was also the bandwagon effect, whereby many simply wanted to be seen as supporting the expected winner.

There was a certain irony in Aristide's successful electoral bid. He decided to contest the elections in response to the candidacy of Lafontant, but remained in the race even after Lafontant was declared ineligible. He was also most critical of the provisional government and the military, although in the end it was their efforts that provided the environment in which his candidacy could succeed.

Aristide's challenges include the need to establish the rule of law as embodied in the 1987 Constitution. The new government must also begin the task of consolidating democracy, which, coupled with the need to immediately address enormous economic and social problems, will put heavy demands on the new leadership in Port-au-Prince.

Perhaps for the first time in Haiti's long history, the new government will be able to draw upon a reservoir of support and goodwill at home and abroad to forge a new beginning for its people. In meeting the nation's challenges, President Aristide must share some of the responsibilities with his designated prime minister, René Préval, and cabinet. Moreover, the newly elected members of the National Assembly will play important roles in meeting the country's challenges. The new legislators, many of whom are members of the president's party, represent specific constituencies; this may, at times, put them at odds with the chief executive.

Demonstrating that a democratic system is capable of providing the necessities of life will be essential to the establishment of a truly democratic culture in Haiti. President Aristide's commitment to justice and the rule of law provides opportunities to rebuild and reshape Haiti's judicial system. Freedom of expression and tolerance and encouragement of political pluralism will be key elements of this enormous undertaking.

Given its performance during the election period, the armed forces of Haiti earned renewed respect. Despite this tangible commitment to democracy, it should not be assumed that all of its members are now democrats. Upon assuming office, President Aristide called for sweeping leadership changes in the army that provide unparalleled opportunities to rebuild and recast this important institution of Haitian society.

Haitians now have a democratically elected government that affirms its commitment to "justice, transparency and participation." Recognizing that the December 1990 elections alone did not signal the arrival of democracy, the courageous people of Haiti have demonstrated their desire to build a democratic society. They deserve the continued respect, encouragement and support of the international community in this endeavor.

The role that international observers played in the Haitian election process also deserves mention. In 1987, the 30-member NDI-sponsored international delegation was the largest observer group present for the elections. This time, the United Nations and the Organization of American States, both of which played important roles in monitoring the February 1990 Nicaraguan elections, assumed major responsibilities in observing the Haitian elections. In doing so, the UN and OAS extended the rationale for observing elections in a sovereign country beyond the justification of helping resolve a regional conflict, which had been used in the case of Nicaragua. There was no regional conflict affecting the situation in Haiti. There was, however, an extraordinary humanitarian need to assist in the establishment of a government whose legitimacy derived from the popular will and not the barrel of a gun.

In another respect, the UN and OAS Haiti election observer missions broke new ground. Both organizations provided significant technical assistance to the Haitian authorities, whereas in Nicaragua their role was limited to observation and mediation. For the first time, the UN provided security advisors to the Haitian government, a decision that provoked a major debate within the organization but one that proved critical in promoting the electorate's confidence in the process.

The assistance of foreign governments in support of the election process should also be noted. They made significant contributions demonstrating a commitment to the democratic process in Haiti and highlighting the growing support network for free and fair elections among the democratic community of nations.

The 1990 Haitian election experience offers several valuable lessons for observers. First, pre-election missions, which were designed to encourage participation in the elections and to help ensure that election-related problems were addressed, contributed to the efficacy of the observation process. The Council/NDI effort began in May, more than seven months before the elections. This early presence provided reassurance to Haitian political leaders who, at the time, were questioning the value of participation. The participants in the pre-election missions assured the Haitians that they would monitor all phases of the election and would be prepared to denounce the process if the government reneged on its commitments. Subsequent delegations focused on issues pertaining to a secure election environment and recommended strongly that the UN grant the Haitian government's request for security advisors.

Second, the observers had to balance an understanding of the difficult circumstances under which the elections were taking place with an application of objective and internationally recognized standards for evaluating elections. This was not always easy in the Haitian context. While the campaign environment was better than many had forecast, questions relating to the manner in which certain candidacies were declared ineligible and the decision to force the retirement of two Supreme Court justices immediately before the elections could, under other circumstances, have been viewed as inappropriate efforts to politicize the legal regime governing the conduct of the elections. There also were serious administrative problems on election day and during the counting process, the precise magnitude of which proved impossible to estimate. By noting these problems in this report, the delegation does not question in any way, the legitimacy of the elections, but instead seeks to highlight the challenges confronting the Haitian authorities as they institutionalize the governmental system established by the 1987 Constitution.

Third, observers had to understand the limitations of their role. In offering a critique of the election law or of administrative procedures, observers were careful to avoid the perception that they were intervening in the internal affairs of a sovereign nation. At times, maintaining a balance proved difficult. As indicated above, there were many requests for hands-on material and technical assistance, and for political advice, presented to the observers by different segments of Haitian society. Observers responded to these requests by advising the CEP before, on and after election day, by providing communications assistance to the CEP and, in some cases, by helping BIV officials transport materials to and from the BEC and BED offices on election day. While it is not always easy to draw a line between assistance and intervention, particularly when the administrative process breaks down as it did in parts of the country on election day, there were no significant complaints presented following the elections from those who believed that observers overstepped their bounds.

Fourth, observer groups should, whenever possible and feasible, coordinate their efforts to ensure maximum coverage of the election. The role played in Haiti's election by the UN and the OAS is a model for such future endeavors. In particular, their joint "quick count" was critical in defusing a potentially explosive situation as a result of the slowness of the official tabulation. Prior to visiting polling sites on election day, the Council/NDI delegation consulted with the regionally-based UN and OAS observers to avoid unnecessary duplication.

72

APPENDICES

LETTER FROM
PRESIDENT ERTHA PASCAL TROUILLOT
TO PRESIDENT JIMMY CARTER

Le President de la Republique

SE/PPR: 383

Port-au-Prince, le 2 juillet 1990

President Jimmy Carter
Carter Center
1 Copenhill
Atlanta, GA 30307

Dear Mr. President:

I understand that you have expressed interest in the electoral process now underway in the Republic of Haiti. I am aware of the many contributions you have made to similar processes elsewhere in the world, and appreciate your own efforts here in connection with the elections of November, 1987.

I sincerely welcome your interest, and would like to invite you to visit Haiti either July 20-21 or July 25-26 so you may become reacquainted first hand with the country. Such a visit would permit you to familiarize yourself with the electoral process now envisaged. This visit also would provide an excellent opportunity to discuss with me, the electoral council, and other institutions the assistance you might contribute to the free, secure, and credible elections we so earnestly desire, including the possibility of a special observer mission.

Sincerely,

Ertha Pascal TROUILLOT
President

DELEGATION ARRIVAL STATEMENT

Honorable Jimmy Carter

Port-au-Prince, Haiti
July 25, 1990

I am pleased to come to Haiti at the invitation of President Ertha Pascal Trouillot to discuss the electoral situation. During the last four years, the hopes of Haitians for liberty and democracy were raised several times, and each time they were dashed. Today I share the hopes of the Haitian people that this electoral process will be safe and free, and that the will of the people will be supported.

I am here in my capacity as Chairman of the Council of Freely-Elected Heads of Government, based at the Carter Center of Emory University, which includes 19 former and current heads of government in the Western Hemisphere. Joining me in this delegation are Dennis Smith, the Chief Electoral Officer of Barbados, who is representing Prime Minister Erskine Sandiford of Barbados; Marc Lalonde, who was a member of the Canadian Parliament and Finance Minister among many other portfolios, representing former Prime Minister Pierre Trudeau; and Dr. Robert Pastor, professor at Emory University and director of the Carter Center's Latin America and Caribbean Program. Our delegation is co-sponsored by the National Democratic Institute for International Affairs (NDI). We will be working with Lionel Johnson, Senior Program Officer of NDI.

A free election is not possible unless clear and concrete measures are adopted to assure the complete security of all voters. President Trouillot has requested observers and a security presence of the United Nations. It is important that the UN respond positively to this request, particularly as it is supported by Haiti's CARICOM neighbors. But if the UN declines, then other alternatives are required, and I will explore these with the President, senior military leaders, and leaders of different political parties.

Appendix III

LETTER FROM
PRESIDENT ERTHA PASCAL TROUILLOT TO
UN SECRETARY JAVIER PEREZ DE CUELLAR

{Translated from French}

The Provisional President of the Republic

Port-au-Prince
September 14, 1990

His Excellency
Javier Perez de Cuellar
Secretary General
of the United Nations

Mr. Secretary General:

I have the honor of confirming the terms of the request provided in letters dated June 23 and August 9, 1990 regarding assistance to the Haitian Government for the organization of the next general elections.

Aside from the assistance to the Provisional Electoral Council that has already commenced, and that I wish to continue, my government maintains its two-fold request for support for the Haitian electoral process: observation and verification of this process; and assistance with the development of an electoral security plan, as well as observation of its implementation.

It is understood that the security plan's civilian aspects will be similar to the UN's and would include:

a) A permanent network of approximately 50 observers who would arrive in Haiti prior to voter registration, and would remain until after the elections.

b) Reserve teams at the time of the elections and if possible, during voter registration, numbering approximately 100 observers. Coordination with the OAS is envisioned.

The security aspects of the operations would include:

a) Assistance to the Election Security Coordinating Committee.

b) Observation of the implementation of the security plans by specialized personnel, that is, by the observers with experience in the area of public order, the number of which will be determined.

It is clear, in the eyes of the Haitian government, that these observers will not in any way, be affiliated with the Blue Berets or other peacekeeping forces. The sole responsibility in this area is that of the Armed Forces of Haiti.

The mission of the experts is limited to assistance to the Coordinating Committee in the development of a security plan and the observation and implementation of the measures provided in the plan.

The experts (military personnel or members of military institutions specialized in the maintenance of internal public order) will not be permitted during their entire mission in Haiti to carry firearms, neither in instances of unrest nor for their personal security.

Their presence will terminate as soon as the elections are completed.

I state that this request is supported by all the government institutions concerned with the orderly and peaceful conduct of the election process.

I reiterate to you the gratitude of the Haitian government for your continued efforts in meeting the Haitian request, and I renew, Mr. Secretary General, the assurances of my highest consideration.

Ertha Pascal Trouillot
Provisional President
of the Republic

Appendix IV

DELEGATION ARRIVAL STATEMENT

Honorable Jimmy Carter

Port-au-Prince, Haiti
September 20, 1990

I am pleased to return to Haiti to discuss the electoral situation with President Ertha Pascal Trouillot, the Electoral Commission, and with General Herard Abraham. I am here because I am convinced that the vast majority of the people of Haiti want free elections, and I am here as Chairman of the Council of Freely-Elected Heads of Government and as the head of a delegation that is co-sponsored by the National Democratic Institute for International Affairs to demonstrate my solidarity with them.

It is clear that there is a small minority of people in this country who do not want elections and are determined to undermine those who do. This small group cannot be allowed to deprive this proud nation of its rightful destiny, to join the march toward democracy that has moved across Latin America and the Caribbean.

The international community of democratic nations supports Haiti and is searching for the best way to assist the election process. I must admit that I am disappointed at how slow the United Nations has been to respond to President Trouillot's request, but I believe a positive response is coming soon.

Today, I have consulted with Jamaican Prime Minister Michael Manley, Foreign Minister David Coore, and former Prime Minister and current leader of the Jamaican opposition, Edward Seaga. I am pleased to report that there is a bipartisan consensus in Jamaica that wants to help Haitian democracy, and we discussed ways that Jamaica and other CARICOM nations will be supporting the electoral process here.

I also met with Venezuelan President Carlos Andres Perez and former President Rafael Caldera, and there again, I am pleased to report there is a bipartisan consensus that wants to support Haitian democracy. We are pleased that President Perez has asked Dr. Beatrice Rangel, the Vice Minister of the Presidency, to be his personal representative and a member of our delegation. Other members of our delegation are my wife; Dr. Robert Pastor, director of the Latin American and Caribbean Program of the Carter Center of Emory University; and Lionel C. Johnson, Senior Program Officer, of the National Democratic Institute for International Affairs.

President Perez told me that he is ready to conclude negotiations with Haiti to be a party to the San Jose agreement so that it can receive very soon oil at subsidized prices. If Haiti has a free election, he told me, this is the first step toward a much deeper commitment by Venezuela to help this country.

Without free elections, Haiti cannot have peace or develop. The democratic community of the hemisphere is ready to welcome Haiti as a full member. In our meetings with leaders in Port-au-Prince, we hope to learn of the timetable for the election. We hope to learn of ways that the leaders of Haiti will demonstrate their support for free elections. We hope to hear from the military their strategy to protect the Haitian people when they register and vote. We will be visiting Gonaives to listen to the views of the people about the elections.

Prime Minister George Price of Belize, who is Vice Chairman of the Council, has informed me that he will lead a delegation to Haiti soon after registration begins. Only the Haitian people can hold free elections, but we are here to show our support for your democratic aspirations.

THE NEW YORK TIMES, MONDAY, OCTOBER 1, 1990

Haiti's Election Needs Help

By Jimmy Carter

ATLANTA

Free elections earlier this year in Nicaragua, the Dominican Republic and even Panama provide clear evidence that democracy is following tortuous, but steadily progressive paths in the hemisphere. Haiti is now moving toward an election in December, but to succeed it needs the full support of the international democratic community.

The Council of Freely Elected Heads of Government, of which I am chairman, played a key role in making democratic balloting possible in these earlier elections. Based on that experience, I believe that the Haitian election, in which the council is already deeply involved, may be the most difficult and dramatic of all.

Haiti is proud of its history as the second oldest independent nation in this hemisphere and the oldest black republic in the world. But for 186 years Haitians' lives have been filled with oppression and poverty. Even in recent years, after finally overthrowing the Duvalier dictatorship on Feb. 7, 1986, the citizens have been plagued with a succession of abortive efforts to find freedom.

As recently as Nov. 29, 1987, an election was called to fulfill promises made in their post-Duvalier constitution. Citizens who lined up to vote were mowed down by fusillades of terrorists' bullets. Military leaders, who had either orchestrated or condoned the murders, moved in to cancel the election and retain control of the Government. Two months later, these generals conducted an "election" that was boycotted by almost all the previous candidates and in which fewer than 4 percent of the people voted; the victor was peremptorially removed when he dared to exert some independence as president.

Earlier this year, after another general was forced out of office, an interim Government was formed, with Supreme Court Justice Ertha Pascal Trouillot as Acting President. Her primary goal has been to bring

Jimmy Carter, the former President, is chairman of the Carter Center of Emory University.

about a successful election.

The obstacles are formidable but not insurmountable. There is a constitutionally established electoral council that has already had to postpone the November election date. However, voter registration is now rescheduled to begin Oct. 5, and elections are to be held Dec. 16.

During my most recent visit to Haiti, two weekends ago, council leaders reported that for the first time they are receiving support from the colonels and other mid-level officers in all regions. They now have assurances of about half the financing needed for the election, with a fighting chance to meet their other needs.

In August, when the Council of State declared all her decisions null

The foes of democracy are back.

and void, President Trouillot survived only after receiving support from the army commander-in-chief, Gen. Herard Abraham. He and the President have been widely and perhaps justifiably criticized for their failure to investigate several political crimes, including the assassination of a member of the Council of State and a labor leader in a Port au Prince hotel. Even more criticism has been leveled against them because of the return to Haiti of two powerful men whose apparent goals are to intimidate the people and to prevent the holding of an election.

One is Gen. Williams Regala, whom many hold responsible for the election day murders in 1987. The other is Roger Lafontant, a notorious leader in the last Duvalier regime whose name still strikes terror among Haitians who know of his former misdeeds. Their presence symbolizes the ineffectiveness of the Government and casts doubt on the ability of the army and police to protect citizens during the coming election period.

Economic crises also plague the country. The Government is already far behind in fuel payments, and

there is doubt each month that it can raise cash, for transportation and other needs. Unemployment may be as high as 80 percent, foreign investments are scarce and only a trickle of tourists are visiting Haiti's extraordinary historical sites. Paradoxically, these increasingly obvious troubles have awakened among many Haitians a strong determination to improve their political system.

There can be successful elections in Haiti if the U.N., Organization of American States, the U.S. and other nations will support a troubled but courageous people who hunger for freedom, justice and a better life.

The O.A.S. is eager to cooperate if moderate financing is made available. The U.S. has promised several million dollars to help with the election. Canada will provide paper for the ballots. West Germany has indicated a willingness to furnish motorbikes for election workers. Venezuela has offered to sell oil on favorable terms and to make additional contributions of services, supplies and money. It is hoped that other nations will help make possible this long overdue move toward democracy.

A crucial decision next week will be made in the U.N. The U.S. has strongly supported an unprecedented request from the Haitian President in July for U.N. election observers and security advisers. All the Haitian political leaders with whom I met said that such observers will be essential for a free election. The time has come for the U.N. to act as courageously for democracy in Haiti as it has for peace in the Persian Gulf. ◻

UN GENERAL ASSEMBLY RESOLUTION RELATING TO ELECTORAL ASSISTANCE TO HAITI

United Nations
General Assembly

Distr.
GENERAL

A/RES/45/2
12 October 1990

Forty-fifth session
Agenda item 154

RESOLUTION ADOPTED BY THE GENERAL ASSEMBLY

[without reference to a Main Committee (A/45/L.2 and Add.1)]
45/2. Electoral assistance to Haiti

The General Assembly,

Taking note of the letters dated 23 June [1] and 9 August 1990[2] from the President of the Provisional Government of the Republic of Haiti to the Secretary-General, in which the President requested assistance from the United Nations in order to achieve the peaceful and efficient developments of the coming electoral process,

Reaffirming the sovereign right of the people of Haiti to choose and participate freely in the determination of their own destiny without any external interference,

Aware of the efforts of the people of Haiti to consolidate their democratic institutions in the face of the potential for destabilization,

---

[1] A/44/965 and Corr.1, annex.

[2] 2/ A/44/973, annex II.

90-25924 2459Z (E)

A/RES/45/2
Page 2

1.   Requests the Secretary-General, in co-operation with regional organizations and Member States, to provide the broadest possible support to the Government of Haiti in meeting, to the extent possible, the following requests:

(a)   A nucleus of some fifty observers that would arrive in Haiti prior to voter registration and would leave only after the elections;

(b)   Reinforcement of the nucleus at the time of elections and voter registration, bringing the total to a few hundred observers;

(c)   Assistance to the Coordinating Committee for the security of the elections, to be provided by two or three advisers;

(d)   Observation of the implementation of the electoral security plans by specialized staff, that is, by observers, the number of whom remains to be determined, with solid experience in the public order field;

2.   *Urges* the international community and relevant international organizations to increase their technical, economic and financial co-operation with Haiti, in order to support the economic and social development efforts of the country;

3.   *Requests* the Secretary-General to submit to the General Assembly a report on the implementation of the present resolution.

29th plenary meeting
10 October 1990

DELEGATION ARRIVAL STATEMENT

Honorable George Price

Port-au-Prince, Haiti
October 16, 1990

Three years ago, in November 1987, I came to Haiti as co-leader of an international delegation to observe the national elections. Due to the tragic events with which we are all familiar, those elections were aborted. Today, as Haiti once again prepares for elections, I am pleased to return at the invitation of Provisional President Ertha Pascal Trouillot and the government of Haiti to observe the electoral process. I hope that our delegation's presence here demonstrates to the Haitian people that the international community continues to support the struggle for democracy in Haiti.

I am here as Vice Chairman of the Council of Freely-Elected Heads of Government, which includes 19 former and current heads of government in the Western Hemisphere and whose chairman is former President of the United States Jimmy Carter.

The delegation is being organized and sponsored by the National Democratic Institute for International Affairs, which has monitored and observed elections in more than 15 countries, including the aborted 1987 Haitian elections. The Institute has also conducted a series of democratic development programs in Haiti since 1986.

Joining me in this delegation are the Honorable Andrew Young, former mayor of Atlanta and former US Permanent Representative to the United Nations; the Honorable Beatrice Rangel, Director General of the Ministry of the Presidency of Venezuela; the Honorable Denzil Douglas, Member of Parliament and leader of the Labour Party of St.Kitts-Nevis; Esteban Caballero, Director of the Center for Democratic Studies in Paraguay; and Lionel Johnson, Senior Program Officer at the National Democratic Institute for International Affairs.

There are formidable challenges along the road to free elections in Haiti. The anxiety felt by the Haitian people regarding election security is fully understandable. It is imperative that steps be taken to assure the Haitian electorate that ballots can be cast on December 16 in a peaceful and secure election environment. During our discussions with political, business, and civic leaders, we intend to stress that only free elections can bring democracy to Haiti,and only a government which is elected freely can command the respect and expect the support of other democratic nations around the world. We urge all Haitian democrats to continue working together to ensure the success of the December elections — for the long-term interests of the nation.

A successful election process is composed of three critical elements: 1) widespread voter registration; 2) the casting of ballots in an environment free of fear and intimidation; and 3) tabulation of the ballots in a system which is open and fair. We strongly encourage the people of Haiti to begin this process by registering to vote during the next two weeks.

TERMS OF REFERENCE

COUNCIL OF FREELY-ELECTED
HEADS OF GOVERNMENT
NATIONAL DEMOCRATIC INSTITUTE
FOR INTERNATIONAL AFFAIRS
ELECTION OBSERVATION MISSION

Port au Prince, Haiti
December 13-17, 1990

The Council of Freely-Elected Heads of Government and the National Democratic Institute for International Affairs (NDI) are organizing an international observer delegation for the December 16, 1990 elections in Haiti. The delegation has been invited by Provisional President Ertha Pascal Trouillot, the Provisional Electoral Council (CEP) and leaders of the major political parties. The delegation includes one current and one former head of government, parliamentarians, political party leaders, democratic activists, regional specialists and election experts from some 12 countries; the United States contingent includes both Democrats and Republicans. The delegation's focus will be the December 16 elections for the Presidency, both houses of the National Assembly, and members of the municipal councils and administrative councils of the communal sections (CASEC).

In the past, the Council and NDI have worked together in organizing international election observer missions in Panama and the Dominican Republic. NDI has also observed elections in Haiti, Bulgaria, Chile, Czechoslovakia, Guatemala, Hungary, Namibia, Pakistan, Paraguay, the Philippines, and Romania. In addition, the Council observed the election process in Nicaragua. The Council and NDI have co-sponsored a series of monitoring missions that have focused on Haiti's security issues and election process in 1990.

The memory of the aborted November 29, 1987 general elections is alive in the minds of most Haitians. The Council for National Government (CNG) was believed to have been largely responsible for the failed elections which were halted due to violence committed by thugs acting with apparent government complicity. The armed forces and police tolerated and abetted the violence perpetrated against unarmed citizens. Thirty-four innocent Haitians were brutally murdered while waiting to cast their ballots. Although the 1987 elections were canceled, an independent election council, embodied in the CEP established by Haiti's 1987 Constitution, emerged as a viable democratic institution. The January 1988 election which resulted in the installation of Leslie Manigat as president, was widely considered to have lacked credibility. Manigat, who was subsequently deposed and sent into exile, was replaced by two successive military regimes before civilian rule was restored in Haiti earlier this year.

There is a consensus in Haiti that the country's future development hinges on the conduct of free, fair and secure elections. President Trouillot assumed office in March 1990 with a mandate to bring them about. The road toward democracy in Haiti has not been without challenges, however. Among them: restoring the level of public confidence in the government's commitment to the democratic process; assuring that the December elections are held in an environment free of violence, fear and intimidation; and securing adequate levels of economic and logistical support for managing the elections.

The Haitian government has, with some hesitation and uncertainty, worked to overcome many of these challenges. Considerable apprehension persists however on the part many Haitians concerning Abraham's and the armed forces' resolve and ability to provide election security. This was further complicated by the return to Haiti in July (in defiance of government arrest warrants) of Roger Lafontant, the former interior minister under Duvalier and head of the infamous *tontons macoutes*; and Williams Régala, second in command of the armed forces under Generals Namphy and Avril (although the two cases are distinct.)

It is nonetheless encouraging to note the increased collaboration between the CEP and the armed forces to provide security during the election process; this kind of cooperation did not take place in

November 1987. Moreover, the decisions by the OAS to send large numbers of observers, and of the UN to send numerous security advisors and observers are cause for added confidence. In addition, observers from CARICOM, the United States and other nations intend to be present in Haiti during the December elections. This strong international presence throughout the election process demonstrates support for Haiti's considerable democratic forces and should encourage a large voter turnout.

In observing the 1990 elections, the delegation is not supervising the elections and we have no intention of interfering in Haiti's internal affairs. The delegation will observe the elections in accordance with internationally recognized standards for the monitoring of electoral processes. It is the Haitian people who will ultimately judge the significance and validity of these elections. The delegation's presence will demonstrate the international community's continued interest in and support for free and fair elections and democratization in Haiti and we will be closely coordinating our efforts with the UN and the OAS. We hope to provide the international community with an objective assessment of Haiti's election process.

The delegation's observations and other credible sources of information will form the basis for conclusions about the elections. Therefore, the delegation must attempt to document its observations and in all instances to distinguish objective from subjective judgments. To accomplish this task, the delegation will meet with government and election officials, leaders of the various political parties, and representatives of other institutions that are playing a role in the election process.

The delegation will begin arriving in Port-au-Prince, the nation's capital, on December 13 and depart Haiti on December 17. On December 14, the delegation will be briefed and provided a detailed itinerary. The delegation will meet with members of the CEP, political analysts, political party representatives and others involved in the election process. To obtain a national perspective on the election environment, the delegation will then divide into teams which will disperse across Haiti's nine departments, including Port-au-

Prince. Upon arrival in the provinces, the teams will be briefed on local political conditions and will meet with election officials and leaders of the contesting parties. On election day, December 16, the teams will visit polling places and counting centers, to observe the general conduct of the elections and to evaluate any allegations of electoral misconduct.

The entire delegation will reassemble in Port-au-Prince on December 17 for a debriefing, preparation of the delegation's preliminary statement, and a press conference. Staff and technical advisors will gather post-election data and evaluate the handling of complaints regarding the elections.

The election law requires that candidates win a majority (50 percent plus one) of the votes cast. If candidates fail to do so in the various races, there will be a second round of elections in mid-January 1991. It is anticipated that a smaller delegation will return to Haiti to observe those elections and assess the process of forming a new government.

Drawing upon the information gathered in the nine departments, the delegation will publish a comprehensive report after the elections. It will be widely distributed in Haiti and throughout the world. The report will include the delegation's observations and an assessment of the issues listed below.

Because of the possibility that casual statements may be taken out of context, delegates should not make any comments to the media regarding their personal observations of the elections until after the delegation has reconvened in Port-au-Prince, all the teams have presented their briefings, and the delegation has issued its formal statement. [See "Press Guidelines" included in this briefing book.] Only then will delegation members have a national perspective on the election process. The delegation statement issued following the December 16 elections should avoid any comment that could influence the outcome of the second-round elections, should they be scheduled in January.

Based on the Council's and NDI's extensive work in Haiti, the following are among the issues we have explored and will be discussing with the entire delegation:

A. Political Campaign

1. Were there any unreasonable restrictions which prevented political parties or candidates from conducting their campaigns in any region of the country?

2. Were candidates or voters subjected to intimidation during the campaign as part of an attempt to influence their votes? What was the response of the authorities to allegations of such intimidation?

3. Did any of the parties present evidence of illegal campaign practices? How did the authorities respond to these charges?

4. At each of the polling sites, did you witness challenges to any candidates? Were these challenges handled in an expeditious and fair manner? Were any candidates disqualified? Were there any legal appeals in connection with such challenges?

5. What effect did the government's election security arrangements have on the campaign?

B. Media

1. What was the role of the media in the elections? Did candidates have access to broadcast media in order to communicate their messages? How did the print media cover the campaign?

2. Did the media demonstrate bias in covering the campaign? Did the news coverage give specific candidates a notable political advantage?

C. Administration of Elections

1. Was the CEP able to administer the elections in a politically neutral manner? Were election authorities independent of political direction?

2. Did the CEP officials act in a nonpartisan manner?

3. Did the safeguards included in the election law prove adequate to prevent fraud in the balloting process?

4. Were voters identified in accordance with the procedures established by the CEP? Were large numbers of Haitians disenfranchised because they lacked voter identification cards?

5. Were voters able to cast a secret ballot? Was there any intimidation of voters by security forces, local leaders, or political parties on election day?

6. Were the pollwatchers designated by the political parties permitted access to polling sites and to the counting centers?

7. Were ballots counted in the manner established by the election law? Were there suspicious or unexplained delays in the preparation or release of election returns?

8. Were there any challenges to the balloting or counting processes?

9. Were observers permitted access to polling sites and counting centers?

D. The Results

1. Were the official results reported in accordance with the election law?

2. Did the various Haitian political parties recognize the results? If not, were challenges filed in accordance with the election law?

3. Was a new government formed in accordance with the prescribed procedures?

DELEGATION ARRIVAL STATEMENT

COUNCIL OF FREELY-ELECTED
HEADS OF GOVERNMENT
NATIONAL DEMOCRATIC INSTITUTE
FOR INTERNATIONAL AFFAIRS
ELECTION OBSERVATION MISSION

Port-au-Prince
December 14, 1990

On behalf of our delegation's co-leader's Prime Minister George Price of Belize, and John Whitehead, Deputy Secretary of State during the Reagan Administration, we are pleased to be in Haiti at this historic moment. On Sunday, the people of this great proud nation will choose their leaders in what we all hope and expect to be free and honest elections.

Our delegation is sponsored by the National Democratic Institute for International Affairs and the Council of Freely-Elected Heads of Government, which George Price and I chair, and which is based at the Carter Center of Emory University. We are an international group from 12 countries. Some of us are Democrats, some Republicans; some Christian Democrats, some Social Democrats — but these are minor differences. What unites all of us and brings us here today is our commitment to democracy and our solidarity with the brave people of this country who want Haiti to be democratic.

This is my fourth visit since July. George Price also led another group from our delegation to observe the registration process. We are well aware of the small numbers of people in this country who have used violence to thwart the democratic aspirations of Haitians. We are here today to say we will not be intimidated by these people, and we express our support for President Trouillot, the Election Council, and General Abraham in their commitment to safe and secure elections.

We hope by our presence to encourage the people of Haiti to vote. On Sunday, the eyes of the world will be watching this country. Our delegation will visit all nine departments, and we hope to see every eligible, registered person voting.

We will be working closely with OAS and the UN to ensure that your vote will be secret and to guarantee that the results reflect the will of the people and are respected.

We are not supporters of any candidate. We support a free process, and we ask all of the candidates to join us in declaring before the Haitian people that they will respect the results of a free election, regardless of who wins.

When a new democratic President is inaugurated on February 7, the world community will embrace Haiti, and all of us will work to ensure that our countries help in the economic development of this country. We have a very distinguished delegation, and I would like to ask each of you to identify yourself for the press and the Haitian people so that they will know that the world stands behind them in their quest for democracy.

TEAM DEPLOYMENT ASSIGNMENTS

COUNCIL OF FREELY-ELECTED HEADS OF GOVERNMENT NATIONAL DEMOCRATIC INSTITUTE FOR INTERNATIONAL AFFAIRS ELECTION OBSERVATION MISSION

December 16, 1990

Team 1A Port-au-Prince
Jimmy Carter
Rosalynn Carter
Ben Clare
Robert Pastor

1B Port-au-Prince
George Price
Beatrice Rangel
Henry Kimelman
Lionel Johnson

1C Port-au-Prince
John Whitehead
Andrew Young
Robert McNamara
Dennis Smith
Larry Garber

1D Port-au-Prince
Azie Taylor Morton
Marc Lalonde
Jim Wright
Jennifer McCoy

2A Gonaives
Christopher Mathabe
Jennie Lincoln

2B Gonaives
Frederick Barton
Kasanga Mulwa

3A Cap Haitien
Robert Rotberg
Karin Ryan

3B *Cap Haitien*
   Lovida Coleman
   Dayle Powell

4 *Fort Liberte*
   Sheldon McDonald
   Alfred Cumming

5 *Jacmel*
   Lester Hyman
   Stephen Horblitt

6 *Les Cayes*
   Francine Marshall
   Lorenzo Morris

7 *Hinche*
   Esteban Caballero
   Sean Carroll

8 *Port de Paix*
   Greg Atienza
   Sergio Aguayo

9 *Jeremie*
   Denzil Douglas
   David Aasen

POST-ELECTION STATEMENT

COUNCIL OF FREELY-ELECTED
HEADS OF GOVERNMENT
NATIONAL DEMOCRATIC INSTITUTE
FOR INTERNATIONAL AFFAIRS
ELECTION OBSERVATION MISSION

Port-au-Prince, Haiti
December 17, 1990

This statement reflects the preliminary conclusions of a 33-member international and bipartisan delegation on the historic December 16, 1990 Haitian elections. The delegation was sponsored by the National Democratic Institute for International Affairs and the Council of Freely-Elected Heads of Government. The sponsoring organizations collaborated on a series of pre-election missions to Haiti, and will publish a comprehensive report on the Haitian electoral process in early 1991.

In observing this election, the delegation was aware that an election process involves not only what happens on election day, but also the pre-election campaign and the post-election transition. With respect to the campaign, the candidates indicated that they had no serious complaints and that the campaign period afforded them an opportunity to communicate their respective messages to the public through rallies, the media, posters and other activities. Most important, while there was some tension that existed and one serious incident of violence, the campaign was conducted in a remarkably peaceful manner.

Regarding the balloting process, the delegation observed hundreds of polling sites in all nine of Haiti's departments. In most polling places visited, the process worked impressively well in providing voters an opportunity to cast their ballots in a peaceful environment. There were delays in opening the polls, but most sites opened by 7 a.m. The pace of processing voters which was slow at the outset, quickened as polling officials became familiar with the process. There were few delays in closing the polls, even where the polls opened late, and the counting at the polling site level was meticulously conducted.

The Provisional Electoral Council is now receiving tally sheets from around the country. It will release the results as they are tabulated. The observations of this delegation around the country lead us to expect that there will be a definitive result from the presidential election.

There were some problems observed at the polling sites, although most of them had been resolved by the end of the day. Most notably, in certain areas ballots and other materials did not arrive on time; this delayed the start of the balloting process in some instances until 2 p.m., preventing many people who wanted to vote from having an opportunity to do so. The source of these problems should be investigated so as to be certain that they do not happen in future elections.

The delegation, however, wishes to emphasize that the problems affected a very small percentage of polling sites, and contrast with the remarkable panorama of a very impressive process. A number of individuals and institutions deserve credit for this impressive success.

The delegation compliments President Trouillot, who under difficult circumstances maintained a commitment to the election process and to ensuring that the government remained neutral regarding the process. Among other initiatives, President Trouillot invited the United Nations and the Organization of American States to observe these elections, and the presence of these organizations contributed greatly in providing confidence to the electorate. This delegation appreciated the opportunity of working closely with the UN and OAS in this effort.

This election posed enormous administrative challenges. The Provisional Electoral Council had to register voters, prepare and distribute ballots and other paraphernalia for five elections, designate and train polling officials responsible for administering more than 14,000 polling sites, and make several delicate political decisions as mandated by the constitution. Despite the problems noted above, the

Council and all of the election officials involved in the process are to be congratulated for their successful and courageous efforts in ensuring that the people of Haiti had an opportunity to participate in a meaningful election process.

General Abraham and the armed forces deserve the congratulations of the international community for assuring a peaceful campaign. The role of the armed forces on election day was truly exceptional, providing a model of civil-military relations in a democratic society, and also providing hope that the military will continue its constructive, constitutional role in the days ahead.

The candidates who participated in the elections at all levels deserve our admiration and respect. They have displayed tremendous courage. The winners should be congratulated on their victories and deserve the support of those committed to a democratic Haiti. At the same time those who were defeated also have a very important role to play if democracy in Haiti is to succeed.

Finally, the delegation wishes to compliment the people of Haiti, who have waited so long to participate in a meaningful election. They overcame what for many were quite real fears of violence to cast their ballots. For them, the dream of a democratic Haiti and a better life can now begin to be realized.

Yesterday's successful elections signal the beginning of the process of solving Haiti's many problems. The country's new leaders will require the cooperation and assistance of many people within and outside Haiti.

The members of this delegation, who came from 12 countries and from diverse political backgrounds, will encourage their respective governments and the international development banks to provide assistance to the new government. In response to requests from the new government, this assistance should be designed to improve the standard of living in the country and to strengthen the political institutions established by the 1987 Constitution.

The election is an historic moment for Haiti, but it is not the end of the road for Haitian democracy. In fact, it is just the first crucial step toward building a democratic system. Of great significance is that the forces of popular change have a unique opportunity to improve the lives of all Haitians within a constitutional system, but these improvements may take some time. What will count is that within a democratic system, such changes will endure.

CONCLUDING PRESS CONFERENCE

COUNCIL OF FREELY-ELECTED
HEADS OF GOVERNMENT
NATIONAL DEMOCRATIC INSTITUTE
FOR INTERNATIONAL AFFAIRS
ELECTION OBSERVATION MISSION

December 17, 1990
Port-au-Prince, Haiti

CO-CHAIRMEN OF THE DELEGATION:

Jimmy Carter, Chairman, Council of Freely-Elected Heads of Government
George Price, Prime Minister of Belize, and Vice Chairman of the Council
John Whitehead, former Deputy Secretary of State (1985-89)

Jimmy Carter: "I think you realize that the task of monitoring and observing an election does not just take place during the election week, but also for a long period of time in advance and also after the election is over. When we first arrived on this visit on December 14, we met with as many candidates as possible, and, I think, all the major candidates. They all certified to us that they had no complaints about the way that the voter registration had been conducted. They had been able to carry out their campaigns without intimidation, without interruption. They had been given adequate access to the media to let the people of this country know what their campaign promises and platforms were. Although there was a great deal of tension and excitement in the country, with the exception of one serious incident earlier this month, the campaign and the election was conducted in a remarkably peaceful fashion.

We've been informed by the electoral council that their first tabulation of election reports will be made two or three hours from now. There's some delay in counting the ballots apparently at the

BED (regional) level, but I think that even this, although delayed, will be done in an orderly fashion.

The observations of our own people, who were in all nine departments, indicated a remarkable consistency in the voting results. We wish to emphasize that the problems that did occur in some of the BIVs (local polling places) yesterday, were corrected in the middle of the afternoon, and this only involved I think less than 4 percent of the total number of BIVs. In general, the people had a chance to express their views in an open an unimpeded way.

Even in nations that have been conducting democratic elections for generations, there are problems, and I think that the Haitian resolve of peace and calm and meticulously detailed work at the local and regional levels has been equal to almost any country we've ever witnessed.

I'm going to call on Prime Minister Price in just a minute to conclude the remarks, but I would like to single out one institution for congratulations, and the deepest thanks on behalf of all the delegations and I think the world community, and that is the military. From General Abraham down to the local village level, the military has performed in a superb fashion. Not only on election day, but in the last few months as preparations were made for this historic event.

As you know, this is indeed a remarkable change in Haiti, compared to what has been experienced in the past, and it opens up a new era for this country to have a close and positive relationship between civilian leaders on the one hand, and responsible military leaders on the other.

In addition, I would like to recognize the members of The National Democratic Institute for International Affairs, which has been the foundation for the work in Haiti, beginning in 1987. They've also been intimately involved in observing the elections with us in Panama and the Dominican Republic.

Prime Minister George Price of Belize, is vice chairman of the Council of Freely-Elected Heads of Government."

George Price: "As President Carter has just said, the tallying process is still going on so we still have to wait for the results. The observations of this delegation around the country leads us to expect that there will be a definitive result from the presidential election.

There were some problems observed on polling day and at some polling sites, although most of them had been resolved by the end of the day. In certain areas, ballots and other materials did not arrive on time, and this delayed the start of the voting in some instances until 2 p.m., thus preventing many people who wanted to vote, from having an opportunity to do so. The source of this problem should be investigated, so as to be certain that they do not happen in future elections, but in general we are informed that most people who wanted to vote were able to vote yesterday.

We would like to congratulate the candidates that participated, and we trust that they will help to work within the democratic process. You, the members of the press, will have a great contribution to make, by helping the newly elected government, when officially declared, to get itself established and to carry out its work for the benefit of the Haitian people. That is why we are here, to strengthen the democratic process, because we do deeply believe that after a democratic government is elected, economic prosperity is needed to stabilize that democracy, and you can do much to help that by the reports you give to the world."

Jimmy Carter: "As I said when we arrived, we are a delegation of Democrats and Republicans from the United States, but we do not represent the U.S. government. We also have Social Democrats, Christian Democrats, and others from 11 other nations in addition to the United States, and I would like to call on my co-chairman from the United States, John Whitehead. He was the Deputy Secretary of State under President Reagan, and is representing the Republican members of our delegation, although we've not had any partisan differences among us on this delegation at all."

John Whitehead: "Thank you very much, Mr. President. It's been a great honor and privilege and very exciting for all the U.S.

members of your delegation here, to participate in this triumphant day for Haiti and to be part of the dawning of a new era for Haiti.

This is the first, not the last day of this new era. Haiti will have many tough problems ahead, and this is only the beginning. I would like to point out that this triumph of freedom and democracy here is part of a worldwide trend that started in the Soviet Union and extended to Eastern Europe and more recently to Nicaragua and now finally to Haiti. I am sure that my own country and all free countries over the world will be eager to help Haiti in its development in the future."

Question: "Mr. Carter, the people are convinced that Aristide is the winner. Do you believe that he will get the support he needs to run this country from the military and from others here?"

Jimmy Carter: "I met shortly before lunch with President Trouillot and with General Abraham. There's no doubt in my mind that both those officials and all that they represent will give absolute and full support to the victorious candidate in this election."

Question: "Do you believe Aristide won?"

Jimmy Carter: "The CEP will be issuing official results beginning in a couple of hours, but the results that we have gotten back from just a few sample polling sites show very strong support for candidate Aristide."

Question: "Mr Carter, was it an honest election?"

Jimmy Carter: "I spent a couple of hours yesterday at the CEP with the major candidates' representatives and with the officials. We estimated that less than 4 percent of the total number of BIVs did not get their materials prior to 10 o'clock, and I think that by 2 p.m. yesterday; all the BIVs that I know about received their materials. About 4:30 p.m., I had a private meeting with the leaders of the CEP and the minister of justice. I also discussed the matter on the telephone with General Abraham, and they all agreed to extend the time of voting into the night for those who were in line by 6 p.m., and to leave the electricity on in Cité Soleil and where the ballots had been received late. Since these were the only irregularities about which I'm familiar, I would say that the election was very fine and was completely honest."

Question: "Do you think the results will be accepted by most of the candidates?"

Jimmy Carter: "Yes, I don't think there's any doubt that the candidates will accept the results of this election."

Question: "Mr President, we've just come from an interview with Mr. Aronson and the White House delegation, and he referred to Aristide as president-elect."

Jimmy Carter: "I met with Bernie Aronson and the delegation as well, and we discussed the mutual findings that we had observed. We were asked by the CEP not to make any definitive judgment until the ballots are counted, but I have not seen any evidence to contradict the expectation that Father Aristide will be successful."

Question: "Mr. Carter, many attempts and threats have been made against Aristide's life, and there are those who say that he won't be able to live long enough to be president?"

Jimmy Carter: "I discussed with Father Aristide a couple of days ago whether he felt the military and the police would protect him. He said the protection had been superb, that he had no fear that they weren't genuine in their commitment to his own safety. Also, he has his own circle of friends and supporters around him who would join in that effort. My own impression is that the people of Haiti are so happy to finally have conducted a successful democratic process, that they will honor the results of the election with great pride and will protect the successful candidate no matter how they might have voted on election day."

Question: "Mr. Carter, would you explain to people why in your opinion, the response to Aristide was so overwhelming?"

Jimmy Carter: "I'm reluctant to make a judgment on the outcome of the election until the CEP makes the announcement. We have only received a very scattered number of responses from about 200 out of 14,000 BIVs, and I'm not willing to make that response. I was not here during the campaign, and I don't know what issues were projected but apparently the people on the streets this morning, whom we had a hard time penetrating, demonstrated the fervor with which his supporters joined in his campaign.   You see that degree of excitement, fervor, and dedication on rare occasions anywhere in the world. I can't comment on the campaign results."

Question: "Who will observe the vote counting after your departure?"

Jimmy Carter: "Most of our delegation has to leave this afternoon, but there're several hundred representatives of the United Nations and of the Organization of American States that will be here until Inauguration Day on February 7th, and they are monitoring this. I might say that the prime ultimate source of results is at the BIV level, and here, not only do the election officials but the observers from the major candidates have certified copies of the results.   If any later discrepancy arises, they will go back to that original count, which may take a few days.   My only guess is that later on today, certainly before midnight tonight, there will be enough definitive results so that CEP can make a final announcement."

Question: "Mr. Carter, your delegation has a lot of influence. If Aristide would be elected president, do you feel that the international community will support him and give him the necessary help that he needs?"

Jimmy Carter: "There's absolutely no doubt that the United States of America will give support to the victorious candidate and this information has already been repeated this morning both by the ambassador here in the country and also by the assistant secretary of state responsible for this entire hemisphere.   There is no doubt that the U.S. will support the results of this election. Beatrice Rangel is a member of our delegation representing Carlos Andres Perez, the president of Venezuela. Perhaps, Beatrice would say what she thinks Venezuela will do."

Beatrice Rangel: "Several heads of state have already begun working to support Haiti.   President Perez spoke with Prime Minister Michael Manley this morning by telephone to discuss ways that the Caribbean and Latin America could help Haiti and encourage multilateral support for economic adjustment programs and humanitarian aid."

Jimmy Carter: "Another delegate here is the former president of the World Bank, Robert McNamara.   Perhaps he can say something about the possible attitude of the international community, including the World Bank, Inter-American Development Bank, and the United Nations Development Program."

Robert McNamara: "During my 13-year term as president of the World Bank, I had never come to Haiti. The reason was that I didn't believe, and the bank and our board of governors didn't believe, that the technical and financial assistance of the bank could be used in the interest of the people of Haiti, under the governments that then existed.   It is very clear to me based on the observations of my associates and myself, that the results of this election, whatever they may be, will reflect the will of the people.   I believe therefore that the government that is elected will be dedicated to advance the social, economic, and political interests of all the people of Haiti.   In that set of circumstances, I am absolutely certain that the international agencies, and that would certainly include the Inter-American Development Bank, The World Bank, The United Nations Development Program, and the IMF, will all provide appropriate assistance to Haiti."

Question: "The electoral law calls for the results for every BIV to be taped on the door, and this was not done. What do you think?"

Jimmy Carter: "I know the BIVs were supposed to tape a copy of the results on the door of the BIV, but I can't certify that has been done, and I assume that you witnessed that it was not done. That is not a fatal mistake. The fact is that the observers of the major candidates have within their possession the results of those individual BIV counts signed by the election officials and also signed by all the other candidates' observers, so if there is any question about a BIV count, you can go to the original document to determine if there is an error. I know it is supposed to be posted. There were some mistakes made yesterday; I acknowledge that's one of them. One of the most serious mistakes was not having everybody begin voting at 6 a.m. at the rules require, but this is not a fatal mistake in my judgment based on results of many observations. This was an election that accurately will express the will of the people of this country.

Andy Young was the Ambassador to the United Nations when I was president. Under Duvalier, he came down to Haiti to try to enforce international human rights standards, and I'd like to ask Andy Young, who has now come back to Haiti under more pleasant circumstances, to make a comment."

Andrew Young: "Let me say that I feel thrilled with the people of Haiti, and particularly the young people who ran the BIVs. I think the election was every bit as efficient as the election we have in Georgia, and we've been doing that for 200 years."

Jimmy Carter: "I don't have time to call on all of our delegation, but I would like to call on Jim Wright, who was the speaker of the House of Representatives in our country."

Jim Wright: "I think I speak for all of us, when I say that we have been grandly impressed with the dedication, the zeal and the determination of the people of Haiti to carry out a truly free and fair election without intimidation, without violence and one that clearly reflects the will of the people of this country. I've seen a lot of elections in a good many countries, and I don't think I've ever seen one in which I have greater confidence that the will of the people has been expressed at the ballot box. I believe all of us who visited different voting locations throughout the country have that same basic feeling. It is a festival of freedom, and we earnestly hope that it will mark the beginning of a new era for this wonderful country and its people, who deserve to have the beginning of a new era."

Jimmy Carter: "Henry Kimelman, was Ambassador to Haiti, during the four years that I was in the White House, and he's been gracious enough to come back and be part of our delegation."

Henry Kimelman: "I'll make it very brief, I subscribe to everything said by President Carter, Ambassador Young, Bob McNamara, and Jim Wright. Thank you very much."

Jimmy Carter: "Okay, since that was so brief, even though Henry has given up his time, I'm not going to waste it, because I'm going to use it to equally good advantage. Ben Clare has come here representing Prime Minister Michael Manley of Jamaica."

Ben Clare: "We concur with the opinions expressed by the former speakers that the elections were fair and free. There were imperfections, yes, this happens in any election, but these imperfections did not affect the plan or outcome which expressed the will of the people of Haiti. As far as Jamaica and CARICOM is concerned, we gave assistance during the election process and we will continue in the future, to assist them economically and otherwise within our capacity."

Question: "Who won?"

Jimmy Carter: "I'm convinced that the people of Haiti have had a chance to express their views at the voting places, and that their desires will be honored when the final results are promulgated. Only the CEP can issue an official declaration, and that will be done for the first time in a couple of hours and then the people of Haiti will know officially what the results will be."

Appendix XI

INAUGURAL ADDRESS
PRESIDENT JEAN-BERTRAND ARISTIDE

February 7, 1991

[Text of address drawn from Foreign Broadcasting Information Service English transcript of Port-au-Prince Radio Nationale broadcast of speech originally delivered in Creole.]

Sister and brothers here; sisters and brothers in the tenth department (Haitians overseas).

Honorable President of the Senate; Honorable President of the Chamber; Honorable Members of the Parliament; Mrs. Ertha Pascal Trouillot, former provisional president; ladies and gentlemen, members of the State Council; ladies and gentlemen, members of the Provisional Electoral Council; gentlemen from the Supreme Court; distinguished members of the Army High Staff; courageous officers, warrant officers, and soldiers of the Armed Forces of Haiti; distinguished members of the foreign delegations; distinguished representatives of friendly countries; ladies and gentlemen members of the international organizations; gentlemen, political leaders, especially from the National Front for Change and Democracy (FNCD) and from the Movement for the Organization of the Country (MOP); ladies and gentlemen from social organizations; dear parents, especially my mother, my sister, my brother-in-law, my nephew, my niece:

Dear friends, ladies and gentlemen: I am greeting you, as you know, as an avalanche member (*l'avalassement*).

We walked as an avalanche [applause]; we marched as an avalanche; we arrived as an avalanche; we are continuing to organize ourselves as an avalanche [applause], an avalanche of love which is covering our country, as well as the tenth department. My heart is basking in this avalanche of love. That is why I cannot help myself from making to you a declaration of my love.

Sister, I love you; brother, I love you. You, who might have some doubts because we have never met fact to face, I come to tell you this, because I know that I love you, and today, 7 February 1991, I cannot help myself from telling you, again and again, seven times 70, I love you. I dearly love you. [Applause] I know that you dearly love me; I know that you all dearly love our beautiful Haiti. All of this is the love which we share with each other, and it is this love that brought us here today to carry us forward to the Haiti that we want to build.

Love and democracy walk hand in hand; love and justice are like a ring on a finger. Love and respect are like fish in soup; love and dignity are like 50 cents and half a *gourde*; love and understanding are the same thing. [Applause] What perfume could smell so sweet! The perfume of love!

Sister, brothers: the clean-up that you did in our country has made Haiti so elegant, beautiful, charming, and orderly while waiting for our avalanche organization to begin its formation.

Yes! To shape up, we walked as an avalanche; we arrived as an avalanche; we are continuing to organize ourselves as an avalanche. [Applause] We are continuing to organize ourselves as an avalanche because as you all know, many hands lighten the load. [Repeats five times, with the people] Let us hold each other's hands like brothers and sisters and say: Many hands lighten the load. [Repeats four times, with the people] What a marvelous thing! Many hands lighten the load. Alone we are weak; together we are strong; tightly united we are an avalanche. [Repeats twice, with the people] If many hands lighten the load, one finger does not eat okra (Haitian proverb). [Repeats three times, with the people]

From 1791 to 1991, it took 200 years of travel to obtain our second independence. When our mother Haiti gave birth to our first independence, our ancestors had said: Freedom or death. [Repeats, with people] Today, 7 February 1991, on our second independence, we are screaming with all our strength: Democracy or death! [Repeats three times, with the people]

On the night of 6 to 7 January, who was standing up? Was it for democracy? [People answer: No!] Were you sleeping in your bed? [People: Yes!] Were you on the streets by yourselves, without the Army on you side? [People: No!] Was the army on you side? [People: Yes!] The Army is us; we are the army. [Applause]

When Pope John Paul II visited us, he had said: The situation must change. Today, 7 February 1991, on our second independence, after Pope John Paul II had said that the situation must change, we are saying that the situation must really change. [Repeats twice] For the situation to really change, the boiler must not burn only on one side. [Repeats sentence] Is the boiler boiling on one side only? Yes or no? [People: No] Would you like the boiler not to boil only on one side? For poor people to share in the country's wealth? [People: Yes]

As time goes by, the situation will really change, because we are organizing ourselves so the situation can change. Thanks to our total mobilization and the guidance of the Constitution, along with Article 291, which we hold in our hands [article condemning *macoutes*], thanks to our organization which will continue to grow roots by creating order, by establishing discipline, by combining participation with openness, thanks to the constitution which will provide inspiration to our senators and deputies, political parties, the FNCD, the MOP, thanks to our respect for the Catholic Church and the bishops, the priests, the nuns, the pastors, the voodoo priests, all Protestant and Catholic people, voodoo followers, and our institutions, without distinction, thanks to these, we are certain of succeeding in really changing our country.

As far as the tenth department is concerned, we do not need to mention it. The avalanche has already begun to arrive home. Tightly united we will sit around the table. Are some people still sitting under the table? [Repeats three times] [People: Yes!] Are some people sitting at the table [People: Yes!] Would you like all of us to sit at the table? As days go by, we will succeed in sitting around the table, no matter what!

The warmth of solidarity opens the flowers of democracy, flowers which are sending out a delicious perfume. We are so happy to contemplate with you this new world. We cannot keep ourselves from thanking you. Thanks to you who are participating in the rebirth of this land. With you, the flowers of democracy will not stop opening. The ties of solidarity, spun throughout our history, rebel today against the reign of dictatorship and oppression. If the Macoute tragedy gave way to the Duvalierist drama; if we kept going from the same to similar, from oppression to dictatorship–today, united with you, we will not have to experience more cruel persecutions. Those of you who were languishing and groaning under repression, and who saw darkness brighten, are awakening today at the doorstep of celebration. You are awakening as an avalanche.

From now on, this historical mobilization and avalanche organization, imbedded with the stamp of Haitian genius, will regenerate the nation. It is at this new cornerstone of history that the decisive emergence of strength asserts itself, now that the people's will is irreversible. It is at this new cornerstone of history that begins the demystifying speech of collective voices denouncing with the deep resonance of the language spoken by the whole population a language of imposture, of stolen speech, gloriously conquered indeed on the day of independence, but perfidiously conjured again later.

The triumph at the 16 December ballot tears off the veil of confinement skillfully draped around the isolation of the people. The failure of the Duvalierist coup attempt on 7 January, as well as the inauguration of 7 February, confirms such a triumph.

The sun of such a triumph is shining for all Haitians without distinction, and almost all Haitians are without distinction. With all countries friendly to Haiti gathered here, we are today united with all the people in the provinces, even though we cannot hold their hands here today. We are extending our hands so that each of us holds another's hands, and together we begin again the shout of solidarity that led us here today.

Alone we are weak; together we are strong; tightly united, we are an avalanche. Again, alone we are weak; together we are strong; tightly united we are an avalanche. Many hands lighten the load; one finger does not eat okra, as days go by, donkeys will stop working for horses. If one finger does not eat okra, whether they like it or not, no matter what, stones in water will get to know the pain of stones in the sun.

A warmest welcome to our English-speaking guests, in our beloved land of Haiti. With the recent free elections that were witnessed by the international community, democracy has found its true meaning within our society. Our task will be to confront many problems: those of corruption, of drug trafficking, of terrorism, of expanding beyond our internal borders. We will be looking forward to close cooperation between our countries, with mutual support and assistance. Democracy in our vocabulary will not be named in vain. It truly will mean justice and well-being for all. The constitution will be the guide for our new, second independence.

The hospitality of Haiti is proverbial. We wish you to feel at home and enjoy our warm climate. Your next visit will surely give us a sense of success.

To my brothers of the Caribbean and of Latin America. To my brother of the Caribbean and of Latin America, I greet you with all my heart. I welcome you to this land, womb of the noblest tradition of our Latin America. I greet you, delegates of those governments which honor this celebration. Your high attendance encourages us to continue in our objective of struggling for the establishment of democracy and of justice in this land.

Never has Haiti experienced such high attendance from Latin America. Such an occurrence testifies to the understanding that Latin America has of the significance of this historical moment which the people of Haiti are living. It is an avalanche moment which corresponds to the long and difficult march our nation, and all of Latin America, has endured to achieve a civilization of mutual respect and participation of all, in a common destiny justice and dignity.

How could I forget my theologian brother of the continent and of the world? With all of you, along with the theology of liberation of the poor, will come slowly the entire and total liberation of man and woman.

Because we love our native language, and because we also enjoy speaking in the language of people who do not speak our language, and who visit us in this moment of solidarity, tying us together with all people, if there were Jewish people here, we would say hats off. If there were Arabic people, we would tell them we are very happy. If there were many Italians, we would say we are walking together. If there were many Germans, at least we would have told them, thank you. If there were many, a crowd of so many, we would have spoken the language of love because no one on earth can live without love, love which brought us here, love in which we are basking, love which we feel when we speak of justice, of participation, of the constitution, of transparency.

Let us give some proofs of transparency (openness). Thus, brothers and sisters, without wanting to keep you for too long, we will sample some transparency about money that has begun to come into the country, even though it is not yet much. We agree that when money comes in, we must know how much money is coming in, and what the government will do with it. Within the next few minutes I am going to tell you what financial help has begun to come in, or is expected to come in, so that you can begin to get an understanding of transparency.

The first financial help that will be received in the country will not come from our foreign friends, but rather, from Haitians living in the tenth department, who are a bank, a source of economic wealth, and who, in giving it, like those who gave their blood, have succeeded in bringing us to this point. Those of us who give must remember the sweat that has been expended all over the country to make it more attractive, to clean it, and to build roads with our hands even when we do not yet have tractors. I, too, come to say that I can also give my meager contribution in another way. This means that the day of the president getting paid 50,000 *gourdes* [$10,000] per month is over.

I am telling the Chamber of Deputies and the Chamber of Senators who have the law in their hands, and all concerned people, that the first thing to do when they think about salaries is to refuse to pay me $10,000 a month because this is a scandal in a country where people do not have food to eat, where people cannot find a job. If you pay me 5 *centimes* [$0.01], I will accept it. If you pay me 10 *gourdes*, I will be agreeable. If you pay me 1 *gourde*, I will agree. No matter how much you pay me, I will accept it. Please make up your mind. Do not hesitate, and decide as necessary.

Concerning our peasants, we do not have enough time to bow to the ground and take on our hats to greet them. I know that it is thanks to them that we can eat, and that I am president today. Potatoes cannot grow in the National Palace, plantains do not grow in the National Palace. There is no corn planted in the National Palace. It is in peasants' gardens that such things grow from their sweat which waters the land when it does not rain. Meanwhile we wait for our agronomists and engineers to join with Haitian and foreign technicians to get water, to work in accordance with the constitution. For now, the United Nations Food and Agriculture Organization says that it can put 1,400 tons of corn seed at the disposal of our peasants so that they can plant corn.

As for children, you know how much we (referring to himself) love children. We could spend all day and all night talking about children. We will just say, however, that [the Republic of] China, the Chinese government, Taipei, is putting $6 million at the disposal of Haitian children, $6 million that can be used toward the work they have already begun to perform in the "Family Is Life" (a shelter for street children Aristide himself created and heads). This money can allow all other children who are drifting in the streets to find work, building with teams of engineers who have begun to work on building the second Delmas Road so that there are not too many traffic jams in Port-au-Prince.

Thus, the children can spend 30 minutes, one hour working on the construction of a road which will help everybody. There is also agriculture in Plaine du Cul-de-Sac. They will have the opportunity to plant seeds in the gardens. I would invite all students, when they go back to school — they will go back to school before long because what has been going on will not go on anymore, must not go on anymore. The children can have just one penny to contribute with China, which is giving us $6 million. Thus, on weekends they could go up to see how the road is being built and help with moving small rocks, carrying some water, and participating in learning to work to build up a society of work, by weeding gardens. This way, children's birds will build progress nests (as received).

China has agreed to put another $6 million at the Haitian Government's disposal. They will lend us this money without interest. The Chamber of Deputies and Senators will decide whether they agree to take this $6 million under this condition and, if they agree, from now on I will be personally proud, I feel proud, very very very proud to say that I remembered how soldiers within the Haitian Army used to live in hovels that deceived the sun, but could not deceive the rain. I remembered how my brothers, the soldiers in the Haitian Army, could not manage to find a way to get what they needed to live like human beings with pride. When they were marking time, they did it Charlemagne-Peraltement.

I greet the army and from now on, I would, if the Chamber agrees, like to show the Haitian Army how the change has begun by telling it — while waiting to get money, much money, very very much money, money that requires time to be counted, for the Army-that we have put this $6 million at its disposal.

There is an electricity problem. At the end of the month we could have had a blackout, but fortunately, with Hydro Quebec International, which signed a contract with me and the German Government, and has agreed to give us $3 million, we believe that we will not have a blackout at the end of the month.

Regarding the Pont-Sonde Road to and from Mirebalais that was being built, the International Development Bank has put $44 million at our disposal so that this road building can continue. OPEC has added $4 million to this amount.

Seventh (as heard), about the petroleum matter, I remember the drivers, I really do. I remember the drivers and the unions. I remember you. As for the petroleum matter, I am very happy that we have the representative of Venezuela, President Carlos Andres Perez, and the representative of Mexico. Both of them have joined hands and have publicly said that they will do all they can so that there is no gas shortage.

Eighth, there are many kinds of minor projects which may come into the country so as to give some help. It is [word indistinct] which will put $11,200,000 (?at our disposal) so that that can be done. There are other projects like the German Government, which has put $36 million (?at our disposal) for this year alone. There are other forms of assistance such as the European Economic Community, which has already provided $144 million over four years.

If I speak of soldiers, officers, and warrant officers, if I speak of peasants, if I speak of children, what will we say for the young people? What will we say for the young people? Young people, do you really feel young? Charlemagne Peralte's young people, do you feel Charlemagne Peralte's blood really flows in your veins? Haitian young people, do you feel that there are courageous young men in the country? Do you feel there are courageous young women in the country? Have you decided to live by tearing up one another? Have you decided to live in dissension? Have you decided to live by killing one another? Have you decided to live in union and close cooperation? Have you decided to live by knowing one another? By supporting one another? By marching forward together? By loving one another? I definitely have good reasons to dearly love the young people.

Timtim! (Creole saying that asks for the answer to a riddle.) Krik! [Audience response Krak! response meaning go ahead]

In general, one does not do that in a speech, but because I am not making a traditional speech, I will tell the young men: Prepare yourselves so that you can greet the ladies like an avalanche. Greet the ladies with a thunder of applause. Greet the ladies. Gentlemen of Haiti, are you there?

I do not hear you, gentlemen. Are you there? Do you feel that the ladies are beside you? Do you agree to support the ladies? Do you also agree to let the ladies support you? One more time, please applaud the ladies.

Well, I am certain that if there were not ladies in Haiti, there would not be life in Haiti. If there were not ladies in Haiti, there would not be this struggle for democracy in Haiti. If there were not ladies in Haiti, there would not be education in Haiti. School is going to open. As soon as carnival is over school must reopen. Ladies, our mothers, all of you peddlers, all of you peasant women,all of you who are dragging around with pitiful slippers on your feet, with a basket on your head, sweat on your face, and ropes around your waists: We men say that we will do all we can to quickly change that. I now reach the last page of the book we have read together today. It is a page of love.

It is a page of love because it is the page where we read the story of a marriage, the marriage of an army and a people, a marriage of danger so often discussed, a marriage of love between the Haitian Army and the Haitian people. Today, the wedding is being celebrated because during the whole campaign we looked at each other. We fell in love. We found a way to meet in our hearts. You (the army) made me understand that you want an engagement between the Haitian Army and the Haitian people; an engagement of unity. Today is the day for that wedding. Today the wedding will be celebrated as it should be. It will be celebrated in love, love that I feel for you, my brother Lieutenant General Abraham. Allow me to tell you before the whole world, before the Haitian nation, I love you. I love you very much, as much as I love the Haitian Army.

Officers, warrant officers, soldiers, when I ponder the river of theology, I learn that authority is to serve others. Jesus washed the feet of his disciples. If I could, I would come and wash your feet so that your feet are not covered in anyone's blood, because from now on, not even one drop of blood should be shed in the country.

To all *macoutes* and *zenglendos*, I am begging you, I am begging you, do not spread discord between our army and our people, which have been married today. Please! It is the law. It is the constitution which is helping such a marriage of love so that we can love each other more every day. Therefore when you the people see a military man pass by, if he is thirsty, please give him some water. If he is tired, please offer him a seat, a home, a bed. If he is exhausted, invite him to rest because, as of today, our military men, the Haitian Army, are our brothers with weapons to protect us against *zenglendos*, with weapons to protect us against *macoutes*. So, since we do not wish bloodshed, I am inviting you, in order and discipline to love the military men. Show them that you love them so that we can walk hand in hand. If I am asking you, who are victims and have victims in your family, I know I am asking you for a sacrifice. Please make it! Please make it! When you love someone, sometimes you must make a sacrifice of love for him. Do you feel you can make such a sacrifice for the Haitian Army? Say yes. Please help me! Say yes. Do you feel you can make such a sacrifice for the Haitian Army? Make it! I encourage you to make this sacrifice because in love I am going to ask the Army to make a sacrifice. I hope that it is in the same spirit of love that they will understand me. I will end this page of love, this page of marriage, with that topic.

Thus, General Abraham, my brother, with all the respect and love that I have for both you and the army, I join hands with you. Together we can make the army a professional army. We can join hands to help the Army feel the self-respect it deserves for its prestige and honor. I ask you, I beg you, my brother, that through this marriage of love with Brigadier General Andre Jean-Pirre, who is promoted to the grade of major general and assistant commander in chief.

It is not an order that I am giving him because the constitution does not give me the right to intervene in the army and give orders to chiefs. It enables me, as the person who holds the title of the army's chief to talk to the general, to get on with the general, so that the general himself may do this favor for us. I believe that the general, who received warm honors, respect, and congratulations, together with the Haitian Army, for the elections that were held, warm honors, respect, and congratulations for having helped us squelch Roger Lafontant's *coup d'etat*, I believe that the general will help us get rid of all that threatens the (Haitian) democracy, by applying the law and discipline so that the Haitian Army can feel successful.

My general, in front of the nation, for peace and democracy, I am asking you, I beg you, my brother, to make the following reforms for us even today in order to provide the Haitian people with what they want. You know you have brothers who shared glory with you in the same battle, who participated too in allowing us to hold elections. I am asking the people — if they believe in me — already, even before you offer me the prize you are offering me for the high command of the Haitian Armed Forces, for our generals, before you offer them this banquet, I am asking you for an act of confidence. You can applaud because what I am going to ask you will be good for all of you.

We applaud, we applaud Major General Gerard Lacrete because he has reached retirement age. General Abraham could help us ensure that General Lacrete can enjoy the joy, honor, and respect that we owe him because he has earned it. We ask that General Serge Saint-Eloi, Brigadiers General Assedius Saint-Louis, Fritz Romulus, Jean-Claude Laurenceau, Roland Chavannes, and Colonel Christophe Dardompre continue to accept glory from us while enjoying the shade of a well-deserved retirement as valiant soldiers who have worked, who have slaved, to deserve so [words indistinct].

General Abraham could promote Brigadier General Andre Jean-Pierre to the grade of major general, and assistant commander in chief Colonel Raoul Cedras could be promoted to the grade of general chief of staff, and with him, Colonel Alix Rene to G1; Colonel Jean-Gracia Delone to G2; Colonel Joseph Florestant to G3; Colonel Frantz Douby to G4; Colonel Michel Louis to general inspector and Colonel Max Maillard to adjutant general.

If these changes are made today, the Haitian Army will be better, the Haitian people will be happy, and the whole world would be joyful because all of those who served would enjoy a great retirement, with honor and respect. All of those who still served would enjoy these same honor and respect, and together we would continue to progress so that the flag we have hoisted today would never be lowered. This way, everywhere, we could say: Alone we are weak, together we are strong, united we are an avalanche. Alone we are weak, together we are strong, united we are an avalanche.

SAMPLE PRESIDENTIAL BALLOT

Appendix XIII

FINAL RESULTS*
PRESIDENTIAL AND NATIONAL ASSEMBLY ELECTIONS

PRESIDENTIAL RESULTS

CANDIDATE	PERCENT	NUMBER OF VOTES
Jean-Bertrand Aristide (FNCD)	67.48	1,107,125
Marc Bazin (ANDP)	14.22	233,277
Louis Dejoie (PAIN)	4.88	80,057
Hubert de Roncerary (MDN)	3.34	54,871
Sylvio Claude (PDCH)	3.00	49,149
Rene Theodore (MRN)	1.83	30,064
Thomas Desulme (PNT)	1.67	27,362
Volvick Remy Joseph (MKN)	1.30	21,351
Francois Latortue (MODELH/PRDH)	.92	15,060
Vladimir Jeanty (PARADIS)	.75	12,296
Fritz Simon (independent)	.62	10,117
TOTAL	100.00	1,640,729

*Source: Provisional Electoral Council as reported.

NATIONAL ASSEMBLY RESULTS

PARTY	SENATORS	DEPUTIES
National Frontier for Change and Democracy (FNCD)	13	27
National Alliance for Democracy and Progress (ANDP)	6	17
National Agricultural Industrial Party (PAIN)	2	6
Haitian Christian Democratic Party (PDCH)	1	7
Rally of Progressive National Democrats (RNDP) (Leslie Manigat's party)	1	6
Movement for National Development (MDN)	-	5
National Party of Work (PNT)	1	3
Movement for National Reconstruction (MRN)	2	1
Movement for the Liberation of Haiti/Revolutionary Party of Haiti (MODELH/PRDH)	-	2
National Cooperative Movement (MKN)	-	2
Independents	1	5
TOTAL	27	81*

*Two Deputy races remain to be held.

OTHER NDI ELECTION STUDIES

- *Albania: 1991 Elections to the People's Assembly*
- *Bangladesh Parliamentary Elections, February 27, 1991*
- *The June 1990 Elections in Bulgaria*
- *Chile's Transition to Democracy, The 1988 Presidential Plebiscite* (English and Spanish)
- *1990 Elections in the Dominican Republic* (co-published with the Carter Center of Emory University)
- *The November 1990 General Elections in Guatemala*
- *Haiti Presidential/Legislative Elections: Report of the NDI International Observer Delegation, November 29, 1987* (Out of print)
- *Nation Building: The U.N. and Namibia (1990)*
- *Pakistan Elections: Foundation for Democracy (1988)* (Out of print)
- *The October 1990 Elections in Pakistan*
- *The May 7, 1989 Panama Elections* (English and Spanish)
- *The 1989 Paraguayan Elections: A Foundation for Democratic Change*
- *A Path to Democratic Renewal: A Report on the February 7, 1986 Presidential Election in the Philippines* (Out of print)
- *Reforming the Philippine Electoral Process: 1986-1988* (Reissued Summer 1991)
- *The May 1990 Elections in Romania*
- *An Assessment of the Senegalese Electoral Code (1991)*

Publications are available for purchase from the National Democratic Institute.